"Written in a down-to-earth style, Tom Hyland's lively and informative
book delivers a user-friendly introduction to the wonderful wine and food
of Piedmont."

    —Kerin O'Keefe, author of *Barolo and Barbaresco:*
    The King and Queen of Italian Wine

"Wine lovers can rejoice in the arrival of a fine book about the Piedmont,
its incomparable wines, its wonderful food, and the producers of both.
Tom Hyland's *The Wines and Foods of Piemonte* takes a sweeping look at all
the wine-producing zones of Piedmont and their cornucopia of pleasures:
not just Barolo and Barbaresco, but other Nebbiolo-based wines, like Boca
and Carema and Gattinara from the hills of the *alta Piemonte*, as well as
Piedmont's so-called "lesser" reds and its whites. He includes as well
telling interviews with wine-makers and chefs, making this book an amaz-
ingly detailed account of Piedmont's gustatory attractions, and a knowing
guide to them."

    —Tom Maresca, author of *Mastering Wine*

Tom Hyland is an American who knows Italian wine – espcially from
Piemonte - much better than many Italian wine-writers and lovers. This
book is an important lesson on the geography of one of the most important of all Italian regions; it also offers invaluable insight into the work of
local producers through lively interviews.

    —Antonio Di Spirito, wine journalist, Rome

Tom Hyland understands the Piemontese culture better than anyone, in
both wine and life. His meticulous research and attention to detail is
reflected in these invaluable stories and interviews. This book allows an
intimate access to the people driving wine in Piemonte. Tom tells their
stories in a complete and beautiful way. Thank you, Tom, for giving them
all a place to be heard.

    If you want to understand Piemonte, you need to go. Please go. If you
can't get there in person, read this book.

    — Joanie Karapetian, blogger, *Italian Wine Geek*

The Wines and Foods of Piemonte

Including interviews with Producers and Chefs

Text and Photos by Tom Hyland

Maps by Alessandro Masnaghetti

Library of Congress Cataloging-in-Publication Data
Names: Hyland, Tom, author. | Masnaghetti,
Alessandro, cartographer.
Title: The wines and foods of Piemonte: including
interviews with producers and chefs / text and
photos by Tom Hyland; maps by Alessandro
Masnaghetti.

The four maps in this book appear courtesy
of Alessandro Masnaghetti.
Cover: Vineyards at Serralunga d'Alba with
snow-capped peaks of the Alps in the dis-
tance. Photograph by Tom Hyland.

*To the grape growers, vineyard managers,
winemakers, winery owners, chefs and
all my friends in Piemonte who have assisted
me in this wonderful journey.*

TABLE OF CONTENTS

Introduction

I have a love affair with Piemonte. Truth be told, I'm in love with just about every region in Italy, but there's just a little more heartfelt emotion about Piemonte as far as my experiences.

It truly is a stunning land. Yes, there are so many locales throughout the country that are strikingly beautiful, but I'll take the view of the snow-covered Alps from La Morra, Serralunga d'Alba or several of the communes in the Langhe and rate that panorama as eye-catching as anywhere in Italy. The fact that meticulously farmed vineyards planted to Nebbiolo, Dolcetto and Barbera are set here only highlights the beauty of this part of Piemonte, as far as I'm concerned.

In the pages that follow, I'll talk in great detail about the wines of Piemonte, from sparkling to sweet, with plenty about the whites and of course, the magnificent reds. There is no question in my mind that more great red wines are produced in Piemonte than in any other Italian region. This includes such iconic, long-lived offerings such as Barolo and Barbaresco of course, but also other examples of Nebbiolo from northern Piemonte, such as Boca, Gattinara and Ghemme. Then there are the delightful, medium-bodied reds such as Dolcetto and Barbera that have become major successes in markets around the world as well as local red varieties such as Grignolino, Ruché and Freisa that are so dis-

Bottle of Francesco Rinaldi Barolo Cannubi.

tinctive as well as charming; you won't find much written about these traditional wines in the major wine publications, but they're just as much a part of the Piemonte wine scene as their more famous counterparts.

Then there is the food that accompanies these wines. One can argue about the quality of wines from other regions in Italy, but there can simply be no argument over the thought that nowhere in the country are there are as many excellent restaurants that create *piatti* that are as flavorful, honest and inspired by the local wines as there are in Piemonte. This isn't just my opinion; I've talked to many Italian wine producers about this and they agree that Piemonte is the best region in which to experience local foods and wines paired together. It's gastronomic heaven!

It's important to note that you can enjoy a great meal and great wines without spending a lot of money in Piemonte. Yes, there are more than two dozen Michelin-starred *ristoranti* in Piemonte, but for me, the heart and soul of this region's dining experience are the more humble *trattorie* and *osterie* that are situated in small towns and large cities throughout. While we often must settle for "good enough" in today's world, thankfully that philosophy is not part of the Piemontese mindset. In this region, you can enjoy marvelously prepared dishes with local wines for a modest charge; you get a tremendous value for your money when dining in Piemonte.

A typical example was the *ravioli di ricotta e spinaci con code di gamberi e zucchini saltate* (ravioli of spinach and ricotta cheese with shrimp and zucchini) I enjoyed (to say the least) for a grand total of 12 Euro at La Rosa dei Vini, an unassuming, but excellent trattoria, situated off a small road in the commune of Serralunga. I paired this with a glass of Arneis; combined with the view of Nebbiolo vineyards just a few hundred meters away—well this Monday afternoon lunch was *settimocielo*—seventh heaven!

In this book, my focus will be on the wines of Piemonte, but you just can't travel to or discuss this region without mentioning the local foods—I don't care how much of a wine geek you

Tajarin, a classic handmade pasta of Piemonte.

are. Wines from everywhere are meant to be enjoyed with food; this is especially true in Piemonte. So when a mention of Arneis or Timorassso-two of the region's finest whites-comes up, I want to know what to pair these wines with; the same for red wines. Again, there is so much variety in the red wines—a Barolo would be ideal with game, for example, but it would certainly overpower a simple dish of *tajarin* or an *insalata* of chicken; for these dishes a Dolcetto or perhaps a Freisa would be a better option.

My focus on the region's foods will be based in a large part on interviews with wine producers as well as chefs; I want the reader to learn directly from these professionals about pairing Piemontese wine with local foods. Many books have been written about the greatest wines and wine producers of this region, but little has been penned about *i ristoranti* and the chefs. I wanted to make certain their voices were heard, as their insight into local ingredients bring out the best in these glorious wines. I hope you will enjoy these interviews.

I must note that I have not included detailed essays about Piemontese food, such as the various types of rice as well as *formaggi*; I love the different forms of *toma* and of course *Robiola di Roccaverano* (especially the ones made exclusively from goat's milk). This is one of Italy's greatest cheeses, one that can stand side by side with Parmigiano-Reggiano, Grana Padano, Bitto or Mozzarella Bufala on the quality platform.

Hazelnuts are a major product of Piemonte; you don't have to go very far within the Barolo production zone to see a field or grove of hazelnut trees (you'll also see a number of Barolo producers selling hazelnuts in their *cantine*). Then you have wonderful fruits in the region, especially strawberries and peaches.

I do believe that there will be enough in this book to give the reader an overview of the wines of Piemonte, from famous to neglected. You will also get great insight into how some of the region's finest chefs think and work; that to me is something that is rarely treated in wine books. Ultimately however, my goal is to get the reader excited enough to travel to Piemonte and experience these great wines and foods for themselves. So many tourists head to other regions in Italy, while it seems as though Piemonte is more of a destination for the serious wine and food lover. Perhaps I can help enlist some new devotees of this region's vinous and culinary products. If so, my endeavors will be worth it!

Tom Hyland
June, 2016

P.S. Please note that I have written about most—but not all—of the wines of the region. While there are numerous limited production wines that are certainly distinctive, I opted not to write about some of the more obscure offerings, as I believed their inclusion would amount to little more than an exercise in trivia.

The Piemonte Region: its location in Italy. © Alessandro Masnaghetti.

The Wines and Foods of Piemonte

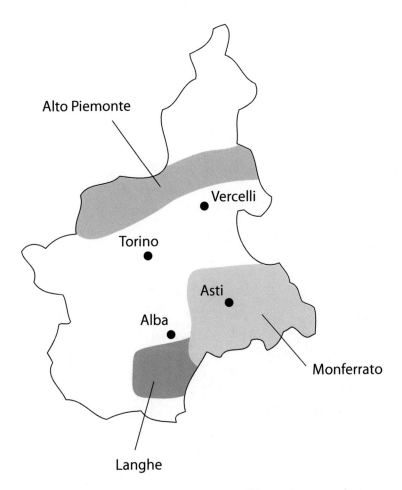

Major wine districts and cities in Piemonte. © Alessandro Masnaghetti.

Major Wine Districts in Piemonte

Langhe

The Langhe district (also known as Langa, the singular form of Langhe), is in southern Piemonte, primarily in the province of Cuneo, with a small portion in the province of Asti. The name of the district comes from the Italian word *lingua*, meaning "tongue," as the shape of the district resembles a tongue.

Wines produced in the Langhe include Barolo, Barbaresco, Barbera d'Alba and Dolcetto d'Alba. There are other wines named simply Langhe Rosso or Langhe Bianco (or with the name of a grape, such as Langhe Arneis). These wines are produced from vineyards in towns such as La Morra; Serralunga d'Alba; Barbaresco; Treiso; Neive and Dogliani. Farther south and west, not far from the region of Liguria, the town of Mondovi is a wine area known for its Dolcetto.

In the province of Asti, Langhe towns include Canelli and Santo Stefano Belbo, known primarily for the production of Moscato d'Asti.

Besides wine, the Langhe is also known for its cheeses and its truffles, especially the famous *tartufi bianchi* of Alba.

The Langhe district, along with the Roero and Monferrato districts earned recognition as a UNESCO World Heritage Site in 2014.

Roero

The Roero district in the province of Cuneo, is situated west of the Langhe, just across the Tanaro River; it is best known for two wines: a white (Roero Arneis) and a red (Roero Rosso, made exclusively from Nebbiolo). Other grapes that perform well in Roero include Favorita (white) and Barbera (red). Wine villages in the Roero include Canale, Castagnito, Monteu Roero, Montà and Govone.

Monferrato

The Monferrato district is located in the provinces of Asti and Alessandria. While several white and red varieties are grown here, it is most famous for Barbera. Important Barbera communes include Nizza Monferrato, Moasca and San Marzano Oliveto. Barbera from here can be labeled as either Barbera d'Asti or Barbera Monferrato. Other notable red wines made in Monferrato include Ruché and Grignolino, which are unique, often rustic offerings, while lighter reds include Dolcetto d'Asti and Freisa d'Asti.

Alto Piemonte

This zone, which will be discussed in greater detail later in the book, is located north of Torino and Novara; literally "high Piemonte," this territory is known for its Nebbiolo-based reds such as Gattinara, Ghemme, Boca and Lessona; these last two usually blended with Vespolina and/or Croatina.

Nebbiolo cluster.

The Wines and Foods of Piemonte

ONE

Nebbiolo

Of the dozens of grape varieties used in the production of wine in Piemonte, the most important without question is Nebbiolo. Barbera is more widely planted; this alone accounts for the economic survival of hundreds of farmers, but it is Nebbiolo that has brought fame and fortune to the region's wine industry.

Nebbiolo is named for the Italian word *nebbia*, meaning fog; this is certainly an apt descriptor, as this is a late-ripening variety that must battle foggy conditions in September and October. As this is a variety that needs a great deal of sunshine to ripen, Nebbiolo vineyards are planted above the fog line—generally from 300 to 500 meters (1000 to 1600 feet)- to ensure capturing the sun's rays.

Nebbiolo is also one of the most tannic varieties in Italy and throughout the world. This is one reason why some of the best examples of a Nebbiolo-based wine can drink well for decades. Balance and depth of fruit—how powerful was a vintage—will also determine the aging potential of a wine made from Nebbiolo; 2006 was a year that resulted in Barolos of uncommon concentration and intensity, so look for the finest examples from that year to drink well for anywhere from 30–45, perhaps even 50 years. Meanwhile a year that yielded wines of average depth of fruit, such as 2009, is not a vintage for the ages; one would be best advised to consume these wines within 10–15 years of the vintage date on the label.

There are actually fourteen different classified wines (DOC/DOCG) in Piemonte that are either primarily or solely produced from Nebbiolo; a few, such as Barolo and Barbaresco are world famous, while others, such as Carema, Lessona and Sizzano are found outside their immediate zones only in tiny quantities, if at all. Some of the wines, such as Boca and Bramaterra are unique because they are usually blended with one or two other varieties, Vespolina and/or Bonarda. These varieties have good to high acidity, giving these wines structure as well as maintaining freshness, yet even with the addition of these other grapes, these wines are still easily recognizable as Nebbiolo.

One of the paradoxes about Nebbiolo is the fact that despite it being a variety that is responsible for some of the richest, longest-lived red wines on earth, it has a rather delicate garnet color; in fact some examples of Barolo from traditional producers that age the wine in large casks can have a pale garnet appearance, not much deeper than a rosé. It surely comes as a surprise to many wine drinkers who are used to the purple tinges of Cabernet Sauvignon or Syrah when they encounter a Nebbiolo-based wine for the first time; they can't believe such a lightly colored wine could be so powerful. (These days, some producers age their Barolo or other Nebbiolo-based wine in barriques, which tend to deepen the color, yet even here, you don't encounter an inky wine that will stain your glass.)

The color of Nebbiolo is not overly saturated nor are the aromas as demonstrative as that of many red varieties. Instead of the blackcurrant and cassis of Cabernet Sauvignon or the zesty blackberry and plum of Barbera, the aromas of Nebbiolo are a bit more ethereal. In general terms, the aromas of a young Nebbiolo are that of red cherry, currant or even wild strawberry with a hint of orange peel or persimmon (this last found often in the wines of Barbaresco). Brown spices such as sage, oregano or even numteg can sometimes be found along with a touch of clove or tar (a classic aromatic descriptor of a young Barolo) and of course, there are the red and orange rose perfumes, fresh or dried. These aromatics often depend on terroir as the wines of Nebbiolo, especially from Barolo, are among the most site-specific in the world; this will be discussed in greater detail in the sections on the various wines.

As for wood aging, the producers of Nebbiolo are often divided on which casks they will employ. Interestingly for Barolo and Barbaresco, the regulations still allow the use of chestnut for aging, although virtually every producer uses oak. Some enologists work with smaller barrels known as barriques; these are commonplace in cellars throughout much of the world, especially in Bordeaux and California. In the section on Barolo, I will deal with this issue in great detail, but for now, let me share the thoughts of Giovanna Rizzolio, proprietor of the remarkable Cascina delle Rose estate in Barbaresco. Along with her husband Italo Sobrino, she opts for the traditional aging method of large casks known as *botti*, in her case made from Slavonian oak. "I strongly believe that these large barrels are much more elegant and fine and respect the character of our region's wines and terroirs. Aging for me is not a process to change the taste of the wines to what I desire, but helping them with slow transpiration of the big *botti* to reach the best balance and development, sort of a slow sleeping. The wine, as the vineyard, must be respected over time."

I love Rizzolio's notion of 'slow sleeping' as I find this a perfect descriptor for Nebbiolo. This variety has been planted in Piemonte for more than six hundred years and while there have been many recent changes in production methods, especially in the larger and more famous zones such as Barolo and Barbaresco, it is the history and heritage of wines made from this variety that define how today's producers work in the vineyards and cellars.

Wines made from this grape, even examples that are relatively approachable at an early age (three to five years in lighter types and vintages) are not what you would describe as being "flash-in-a-pan", showy wines meant for high scores from wine gurus that love spice and sizzle in their red wines. Rather, these

In the upcoming chapters, I will discuss famous wines from Piemonte made from Nebbiolo, such as Barolo, Barbaresco, Gattinara and Ghemme. Other less expensive examples include Langhe Nebbiolo, made exclusively from Nebbiolo grapes sourced from vineyards that are in the Barolo and Barbaresco production zones, and Nebbiolo d'Alba, a 100% Nebbiolo sourced from vineyards in the Langhe not inside the Barolo and Barbaresco zones.

are understated wines that take time to reveal their charms that are often hidden upon release. For a group of wines that can age for decades and can often be decribed as powerful and brawny, many of these wines have a femininity to them, as they display finesse amidst their muscle. In this way, Nebbiolo is sometimes compared to Pinot Noir, and the Nebbiolo-based wines of Piemonte likened to the most typical offerings of Burgundy.

This is an argument for perhaps another day, but indeed, this notion only reinforces the complexities and distinctiveness of Nebbiolo. Change is inevitable over the course of centuries, thanks to climate as well as human whim, but the purity of Nebbiolo has never been argued in Piemonte.

Zona di produzione del Barolo docg
Barolo docg production zone

Roddi

Verduno

Grinzane
Cavour

Cherasco

Diano
d'Alba

La Morra

Castiglione
Falletto

Barolo

Serralunga
d'Alba

Novello

Monforte
d'Alba

©Alessandro Masnaghetti.

TWO

Barolo

Barolo is one of several Piemontese wines made exclusively or primarily from the Nebbiolo grape. Others, including Barbaresco and Gattinara are distinctive wines that beautifully communicate the characteristics of this variety and in the best examples, offer a sense of their origins. They can be long-lived, drinking beautifully some two or three decades after the vintage. Yet Barolo, which does all of these things well, stands alone among the region's red wines.

The name of the wine comes from the quaint town in the southern sector of the production zone, but Barolo can be produced from eleven different communes, the five largest being: La Morra, Barolo, Castiglione Falletto, Monforte d'Alba and Serralunga d'Alba. A majority of the most renowned examples of Barolo originate from one of these five communes, but there are also dozens of first-rate examples from the other six; they are: Verduno; Novello; Grinzane Cavour; Roddi; Cherasco and Diano d'Alba.

Whether the source for a Barolo is a large or small commune, the subject of terroir is paramount to the best examples. Terroir is a term that examines the origins of a wine—the exact site and numerous factors as to why wines from that particular place taste the way they do; combining soil, elevation, exposure to the sun, wind, rain and other things. It is never an exact science of

Vineyards below the town of La Morra in the heart of the Barolo zone.

course, but that only deepens the aura of terroir, especially when it is appropriately applied, as in the case of Barolo.

For the Barolo zone, situated south of the city of Alba, soil is the primary factor for any discussion of terroir. The soils in the Barolo zone are millions of years old, created when this land emerged from the sea when the geological plates of Africa and Europe crashed together. The most ancient soils, known as Helvetian or Diano sandstone, are poor, resulting in wines that are very tannic, while the younger soils, known as Tortonian or Sant'Agata marl, produce wines with less powerful tannins and more floral aromatics. While these soils are sometimes mixed, as in a small part of the commune of Barolo, an easy way to remember what soils are in what communes is to draw a vertical line down a map of the zone. If we look at the map with north at the top, then the communes to the right, namely Monforte d'Alba, Serralunga d'Alba and Castiglione Falletto are dominated by Helvetian soils, while to the left (west) of the map, the younger Tortonian soils are a feature of La Morra, Verduno, Novello and most of Barolo.

Alfio Cavallotto, winemaker, Cavallotto, one of Barolo's
greatest traditional estates.

Thus a communal comparison can easily be made for Barolo. Gianluca Grasso, winemaker at the Elio Grasso estate in Monforte, talks about Barolo from this commune as well as Serralunga. "These are Barolos that are masculine, Barolos that are very
strong with power. They talk to you in the future—they are not for
immediate drinking." At Fontanafredda in Serralunga, winemaker Danilo Drocco comments that "every little valley in Serralunga
is a *grand cru*, a single vineyard with great potential." He reasons

The Wines and Foods of Piemonte

Maria Teresa Mascarello carries on the great work of her father Bartolo at their small winery in the town of Barolo.

that the combination of the vineyards' altitude and exposition to the sun along with the very poor soil, "is the secret of Serralunga," and that a typical Barolo from this commune, "is very rich with full body and a big structure of tannins."

In La Morra, the typical Barolo has much a much gentler tannic profile along with a more floral aromatic presence. "La Morra always makes a Barolo that is more elegant, more feminine with elegant tannins," says Luca Currado, winemaker at Vietti, who

Paolo Manzone produces classically styled, long-lived Barolo from Serralunga d'Alba.

produces a Barolo from the Brunate vineyard that is on border of the La Morra and Barolo communes. "The wines are very elegant with tannins that are round and they become velvety so they are drinkable a little sooner than the others."

A similar style emerges from other communes with Tortonian soils, such as Verduno, Novello and most of Barolo. Interestingly, the famed Cannubi vineyard in Barolo contains both types of soils, resulting in a very unique terroir for this cru. Matteo Sardegna, proprietor of Poderi Luigi Einaudi, produces a Cannubi

The Wines and Foods of Piemonte

Valter Fissore, winemaker, Elvio Cogno.

Barolo as well as another cru Barolo from nearby and notes the distinctive qualities of wine from Cannubi. "A Cannubi Barolo has a distinct minerality and a balsamic character. It is also characterized by its elegance, a balance without equal." He notes that his Barolo from the Terlo cru just a few kilometers away is more fruit forward but displays less of a balsamic note.

The argument of terroir for specific communes can also be broken down into site specifics. Sergio Germano, winemaker at the Ettore Germano estate in Serralunga, points out the subtle

Claudio Fenocchio, winemaker, Giacomo Fenocchio.

differences in the Prapò and Ceretta vineyards he works with in this commune. "Ceretta is more powerful," he remarks. It is at the top of the hill, some 400 meters (1300 feet) above sea level, totally calcaire (limestone) soil, this is full-bodied with a high concentration of tannins. Prapò is slightly lower elevation (370 meters, 1200 feet), with more sand. Prapò is a bit more lean at the beginning, so I age in large barrels (3000–4000 liters), while for the more tannic Ceretta, I age in 700-liter *tonneaux*."

Terroir can be a beautiful "pure" argument, based on location, but there is always human intervention; thus wines from

The Wines and Foods of Piemonte

the same vineyard will taste differently, according to numerous personal decisions from the grape grower or winemaker. Let's look at how a Barolo is matured for instance. For decades, only large casks known as *botti*—ranging in size from 2000 to 5000 liters—were used to age Barolo for several years. Many producers still use these containers, limiting the influence of wood; these "traditional" wines in the opinion of many (myself included), are more honest and better reflect the varietal purity of Nebbiolo as well as the terroir attributes of a site or sites (as in a Barolo blended from several vineyards).

Other producers age their Barolo in small oak barrels known as barriques; the common size here being 225 liters. This practice began in the 1970s and early 1980s when some producers wanted to make a riper, spicier Barolo that would be more in line with modern tastes and would also be more drinkable sooner (for decades, Barolo aged solely in *botti* were often tightly wound wines upon release that demanded a decade or more to round out and become drinkable). Then there are some enologists that use the mid-size *tonneaux*, as in the case of Germano for his Ceretta Barolo, while some, such as Danilo Drocco at Fontanafredda in Serralunga, will use both barrique and *botti* for maturation.

The Best Wines and Cru

Here is a selective list of some of the finest examples of Barolo, both classically blended wines as well as cru bottlings.

Bartolo Mascarello
Pio Cesare
Giuseppe Rinaldi ("Brunate-Le Coste", "Cannubi San Lorenzo-Ravera", "Tre Tini")
Umberto Fracassi
Oddero
Prunotto
Batasiolo
G.D. Vajra "Albe"
Luciano Sandrone "Le Vigne"
Fontanafredda (Serralunga communal bottling)
Ettore Germano (Serralunga communal bottling)
Giovanni Rosso (Serralunga communal bottling)

Cru from La Morra
Rocche dell'Annunziata
Renato Ratti; Paolo Scavino; Rocche Costamagna; Mauro Veglio; Aurelio Settimo; Fratelli Ravello; Andrea Oberto; Mario Gagliasso

Conca
Renato Ratti, Mauro Molino, Fratelli Ravello

Cerequio
Roberto Voerzio, Michele Chiarlo, Batasiolo

La Serra
Roberto Voerzio, Marcarini, Mauro Molino, Gianni Voerzio

Brunate (this cru straddles the La Morra-Barolo border)
Roberto Voerzio; Francesco Rinaldi; Vietti; Ceretto; Elio Altare; Poderi Oddero; Andrea Oberto

Cru from Barolo

Cannubi
Michele Chiarlo; Francesco Rinaldi; Marchesi di Barolo, Serio e Battista Borgogno; Giacomo Brezza; Giacomo Fenocchio; Barale Fratelli; Giacomo Borgogno; E. Pira; Luigi Einaudi; Damilano; Cascina Adelaide; Tenuta Carretta; Ceretto (Cannubi San Lorenzo); Luciano Sandrone (Cannubi Boschis); Cantina del Nebbiolo (Cannubi Boschis); Virna (Cannubi Boschis)

Sarmassa
Roberto Voerzio; Marchesi di Barolo; Giacomo Brezza; Virna (Preda Sarmassa)

Castellero
Giacomo Brezza, Barale Fratelli

Liste
Giacomo Borgogno, Francesco Boschis, Damilano

Terlo
Marziano Abbona, Luigi Einaudi (both Terlo and Costa Grimaldi Barolos)

Bricco delle Viole
G.D. Vajra, Giovanni Viberti

Cru from Castiglione Falletto

Rocche di Castiglione
Vietti; Ceretto; Poderi Oddero; Brovia; Roccheviberti

Villero
Giacomo Fenocchio; Vietti (Riserva); Giuseppe Mascarello; Cordero di Montezemolo (Enrico VI); Poderi Oddero; Franco Molino; Livia Fontana

Parussi
Massolino, Gianfranco Bovio

A by-product of these changes in maturation has resulted in a modification of the regulations for Barolo. Currently, the minimum aging in wood for a Barolo is eighteen months, down from twenty-four. This was altered no doubt to the fact that smaller casks came into play; certainly a wine could be overwhelmed by wood notes if matured too long in barriques, so the *disciplinare* regulations were modified. Eighteen months is the *minimum* aging period in wood for a Barolo, but there are many producers that continue to age their wine in casks for twenty-four months or even longer. Barolo is generally released at four years of age, (the 2010s were released in 2014, e.g.), while a Barolo Riserva, which has longer overall minimum aging regulations at the winery, is released six years after the vintage date.

Today, a greater number of the area's producers make cru Barolo, wine from a single vineyard. There are more than 175 in the overall zone, with La Morra and Serralunga each having 39 separate cru, while on the other end of the spectrum, both Cherasco and Roddi have only one; these sites—ranging from ten acres to more than one hundred-are generally divided up among several owners (though there are a few vineyards under a single winery's control).

Yet for years, the norm in the zone

The Wines and Foods of Piemonte

was to make a Barolo blended from a number of vineyards and in some instances, different communes. Certainly the appeal of terroir from a single site helps explain the shift toward cru Barolo (not to mention more limited production as well as higher prices and arguably more media attention), but there are still producers that take pride in the classic tradition of a Barolo blended from several sources. Producers such as Fontanafredda and Ettore Germano in Serralunga make a Barolo sourced from a several vineyards within this commune; these are lighter wines than their cru offerings of course, but these communal Barolos can be enjoyed sooner than their counterparts, offer excellent value and in an oustanding vintage such as 2010, are quite special.

Then there are producers that remain true to the historic way of producing Barolo sourced from more than one commune; two of the best on the market today are from Pio Cesare and Bartolo Mascarello. The classic Pio Cesare Barolo is sourced from several leading cru in Serralunga, Grinzane Cavour and Novello along with other sites from Castiglione Falletto and Monforte, while the Bartolo Mascarello Barolo is a blend of fruit from Barolo and La Morra.

The Cesare bottling year in and year out is an excellent wine and serves as a nice introduction to Barolo as well

Bricco Boschis
Cavallotto (includes San Giuseppe Riserva)

Vignolo
Cavallotto

Pira
Roagna (La Rocca e la Pira)

Monprivato
Giuseppe Mascarello

Cru from Monforte d'Alba
Bussia
Aldo Conterno (Gran Bussia, Cicala, Colonnello, Romirasco); Bussia Soprana (Bussia, Colonello, Gabutti della Bussia); Poderi Oddero (Vigna Mondoca); Barale Fratelli; Giacomo Fenocchio; Cascina Ballarin; Angelo Germano (Vigna Mondoca); Poderi Ruggeri Corsini (Corsini)

Ginestra
Paolo Conterno; Elio Grasso (Casa Maté); Domenico Clerico (Ciabot Mentin); Conterno Fantino (Sorì Ginestra and Vigna del Gris), Cascina Chicco

Gramolere
Fratelli Alessandria, Giovanni Manzone

Castelletto
Giovanni Manzone; Gigi Rosso; Josetta Saffirio (Persiera); Marziano Abbona (Pressenda)

Gavarini
Elio Grasso (Gavarini Chiniera)

Cru from Serralunga d'Alba
Lazzarito
Fontanafredda; Ettore Germano; Vietti; Guido Porro (Lazzairasco, Vigna Santa Caterina)

Vigna Rionda
Massolino; Giovanni Rosso
   (Tommaso Canale); Ettore
   Germano; Luigi Pira; Poderi
   Oddero; Roagna

Prapò
Ceretto, Ettore Germano,
   Schiavenza, Mauro Sebaste

Ceretta
Giovanni Rosso; Ettore
   Germano; Luigi Baudana,
   Schiavenza

Margheria
Massolino, Azelia, Luigi Pira

Badarina
Bersano, Bruna Grimaldi (Vigna
   Regnola)

Meriame
Paolo Manzone, Riikka Sukula

Sorano
Ascheri (Sorano and Sorano
   Coste e Bricco), Claudio Alario

Boscareto
Batasiolo, Ferdinando
   Principiano

Briccolina
Batasiolo (Corda della
   Briccolina), Rivetto

Parafada
Massolino, Poderi Sorì

Baudana
Luigi Baudana, Cascina Adelaide

as an example of the house's style with this wine; it is also a nice lead-in to their cru Barolo from Ornato in Serralunga (this site is also a source of fruit for their classic bottling). As for the Bartolo Mascarello Barolo, it is a stunning wine and certainly one of the most famous and revered of its type. For more than five decades, *signore* Mascarello produced only one Barolo in a vintage, a wine that was blended from his family's holdings in four separate vineyards: three in Barolo (Cannubi, San Lorenzo and Rué) and from Rocche in La Morra (now known as Rocche dell'Annunziata).

Masacarello was carrying on the approach of his father, who first made Barolo in 1918, that blending fruit from various sites would create the finest wine, one with great complexity, with a sense of balance and harmony and not power or intensity. Mascarello always aged his wine in *botti*, so as to emphasize the character of Nebbiolo and downplay the wood notes. But it was more than that; Mascarello along with other great traditionalists such as Beppe Rinaldi and Elio Grasso believed that aging in large casks resulted in a Barolo that was slower to evolve, but one that would reward the patience of the buyer; these wines stand the test of time and peak at 25–50 years, depending on the strength of the vintage. Like the man himself, the Barolos of Bartolo Mascarello were not flashy or attention grabbing; rather they were—and continue to be—graceful and honest. Mascarello passed away in 2005 at the age of 78; today his daughter Maria Teresa continues to produce one Barolo each vintage in the same manner; this has become a Barolo that is truly a reference point.

As with all types of businesses, Barolo producers deal with a different world today than their parents or grandparents. Climate change–"the biggest change in Barolo today," according to Mariacristina Oddero of the Poderi Oddero estate in La Morra—has affected harvest dates, as Nebbiolo in this zone is now harvested in mid-October rather than late October or early November, as was the norm more than twenty years ago. Alcoholic content is different; a 1990 Conca Barolo from Renato Ratti was 13% alcohol, while the 2010 is at 14% alcohol—and 1990 was a warm growing season! As noted previously, the wines are more approachable today as compared to three or four decades earlier; this a result of both the weather as well as practices in the vineyard and the cellar.

But are today's Barolos as good as those from the 1960's, '70s and '80s? Will they age as long? Many producers would answer yes to both questions. "The wines today are better made than

Fontanafredda
Fontanafredda (La Rosa)

Ornato
Pio Cesare, Palladino

Falletto
Bruno Giacosa (Barolo Falletto and Le Rocche del Falletto)

Francia
Giacomo Conterno (Vigna Francia and Monfortino Riserva)

Cru from Novello
Ravera
Elvio Cogno, Vietti, Vajra

Sottocastello
Ca' Viola, Giacomo Grimaldi

Cru from Verduno
Movigliero
Paolo Scavino, Fratelli Alessandria, Mauro Sebaste, Pietro Rinaldi

Cru from Roddi
Bricco Ambrogio
Paolo Scavino, Bruna Grimaldi, Negretti

they were in the past," notes Gianluca Grasso. "In the past, sulfites were higher than they are today." Maunel Marchetti, proprietor of Marcarini in La Morra, comments that "while the yields of today are about the same as in years past, the biggest change is the reduction of pesticides."

As for aging potential, Grasso is quite confident about the Barolos of today. "The wines are going to age as long or longer than in the past. There is only one doubt about the wines we are making today—the corks are not as good as in the past."

THREE

Barbaresco

While Barolo is celebrated as one of the world's greatest wines, Barbaresco, made from the same grape and produced from vineyards only a few miles away, remains a wine that is greatly underappreciated. Yet, Barbaresco is, in the finest examples, a grand wine to celebrate for its richness, singularity and sense of place.

Barbaresco is produced from a small area to the north and east of the city of Alba. There are three communes where most of the wine is made: Treiso, just north of Alba; Barbaresco, just north of Trieso and finally, Neive, just east of Barbaresco. There is also a small zone on the outskirts of the city of Alba known as San Rocco Seno d'Elvio, however, this term is not used on the label as a legal classification. As there are only three commuunes for Barbaresco (or four, depending on your point of view) as compared to eleven for Barolo, it stands to reason that there is much less Barbaresco produced; the total is about one-third to that of Barolo.

Barbaresco must be aged for a minimum of 26 months with at least nine months in wood. The wine is generally released three years after the vintage date or one year earlier than Barolo, which is another reason why the wine is perceived as being lighter than its counterpart to the south of Alba.

A primary reason why Barbaresco is not as brawny as Barolo

has to do with the soils that are dominant in this zone; as these are Tortonian soils, these are younger than the ancient Helvetian, so the tannins are not as strong. That in turn leads to varying production methods for these two wine types, according to Giovanna Rizzolio of Cascina delle Rose, one of Barbaresco's finest producers. "As Barolo has a bigger tannic structure, many winemakers vinify in wood and cement, often arriving at long macerations—some for months! This way will extract more tannins."

For Alessandro Ceretto, who produces both Barolo and Barbaresco for his family estate, "the differences come from the soil, the exposure, the altitude." He does believe that Barbarescos are "more elegant, fruit-focused and fresh," while Barolos "are more concentrated, have more power and complexity," but thinks the two wines are similarly remarkable in their breeding. "When you talk about great terroirs in Barbaresco, some of them are really close to Barolo," he remarks. "I don't consider Barolo better than Barbaresco. I always talk about some terroirs being better than others."

For the remainder of this chapter, I opt not to focus on a comparison of Barbaresco and Barolo, as in the final analysis, it is a bit futile. I love Barbaresco and think it is a great wine, one that has a soul (or *anima*, as the Italians call it); it's a matter of the best producers working with grapes sourced from the finest sites. So let's talk about the most famous cru and the most highly regarded Barbaresco estates.

An absolute reference point for Barbaresco is the Produttori del Barbaresco, located just across from the famed tower of Barbaresco in the heart of the town. This is a cooperative firm (the grapes are supplied by growers who are members), by far the finest in the area as well as Piemonte and one of the most famous in the entire country. Founded in 1958 by a local priest as a way of helping local growers band together for economic survival, the cooperative has grown to 56 grower members that farm 100 hectares (250 acres) solely within the Barbaresco commune.

Today under the direction of general manager Aldo Vacca, the Produttori releases a classic Barbaresco each vintage and in

Vineyards below the town of Barbaresco adjacent to the Tanaro River.

the finest years, also nine different cru bottlings. I have sat down with Vacca on at least three occasions at the winery and tasted through all nine from the same vintage-talk about an enjoyable and informative session! There is a definite thread going through the wines, not only because they are Nebbiolo from vineyards situated very close to each other, but because of the house style, one that respects the tradition of Barbaresco, as the wines are matured in the large *botti*, which limits wood influence, while reinforcing varietal purity. The wines remain for three years in these casks, starting with 25 to 55 hectoliter barrels and finishing in 70 and 100 hectoliter barrels.

The classic Barbaresco is treated in the same fashion and as it is a blend of fruit from a select few of these vineyards, it is a perfect representation of not only the heritage of winemaking in this commune, but also a summary of how stellar this wine can be. I can't recommend the classic bottling from Prouttori del Barbaresco enough; it is also a great value.

As for the cru bottlings, these are consummate examples of the class, breeding and elegance of this great wine. While all nine wines are from the commune of Barbaresco, there are subtle differences of terroir; again, aging these wines in large casks helps bring out the site specific differences. Vacca divides the wines into three separate categories with the Pora, Rio Sordo and Asili being the most approachable upon release (Rio Sordo has been a lovely wine these past few years), while Pajé, Ovello and Muncagota (formerly known as Moccagotta) have "a little more acidity, freshness and floral notes," in the words of Vacca.

The final three, Rabajà, Montefico and Montestefano are the most powerful and longest-lived (my notes on the 2008 Montestefano, tasted upon release in 2013, was for peak consumption in 15–20 years). Vacca notes that these vineyards are the "warmest spots" giving the wines "power and tannin." Tasting through these final three wines would probably convince you that yes, Barbaresco can be as robust and as remarkable as Barolo!

Another great estate in Barbaresco is the previously mentioned Cascina delle Rose. Rizzolio, her husband Italo Sobrino and their sons Davide and Riccardo fashion two lovely offerings of Barbaresco from the Rio Sordo subzone where they are located; the wines are Rio Sordo and Tre Stelle, this last a cru that was created in 2005 when Rio Sordo was divided into two sections. Their wines are remarkably elegant and imbued with great finesse, not only due to their aging in traditional large casks, but also the site specifics as well. Rizzolio points out that these two cru have "very calcerous (clay) soils which give floral aromatics, silky and very elegant tannins and great complexity." Rizzolio compares these two sites with Montestefano, which she claims is "structured with more intensity."

There are numerous traditional producers in Barbaresco, most famously Marchesi di Gresy (at their fabulous Martinenga estate that has produced very long-lived Barbarescos) and Bruno Giacosa, a legendary vintner, whose Barbaresco from the Asili cru is among Piemonte's most famous wines. Other first-rate traditional producers in the zone include Rizzi and Pertinace, a very fine cooperative, both from Treiso, Giuseppe Cortese and Albino Rocca (Barbaresco) and Castello di Neive and Ugo Lequio (Neive).

There has also been a great deal of experimentation in the production zone over the past twenty years with several producers using small or mid-size French barrels; among the best of these are Fiorenzo Nada and Pelissero (Treiso), Bruno Rocca and Moccagatta (Barbaresco) and Fontanabianca and Sottimano (Neive). Another esteemed modern producer of Barbaresco is Giorgio Rivetti of La Spinetta, whose firm is located outside of the zone; his four cru Barbarescos from Treiso and Neive are deeply concentrated and quite sleek.

Of course, no conversation of Barbaresco can take place without mentioning the wines of Angelo Gaja. While opinions vary greatly about his approach in terms of marketing and selling his wines, virtually every area producer of agrees that Gaja did a tremendous amount to help make the name of Barbaresco a vital part of the international wine scene. "Angelo is one of the top ten wine personalities of the world," comments Alessandro Ceretto, who produces cru Barbaresco from Asili and Bernadot. "He is a producer that has been able to communicate to the world that our wines can reach qualities that not many others can achieve."

Angelo Gaja acquired his philosophy of generating the highest quality from his father Giovanni, who set about purchasing the best local vineyards during the 1950s, '60s and '70s; this was at a time when almost every producer was purchasing grapes from negociants. Today, Gaja has several remarkable vineyards in the commune of Barbaresco, including Sorì San Lorenzo and Sorì Tildin.

These two vineyards are the source of his most renowned wines, yet they are not identified as Barbaresco, as they contain 5% Barbera; thus they are labeled as Langhe Nebbiolo. Gaja explains that his choice of including Barbera in the blend was done in reponse to the warmer temperatures—and thus earlier ripening conditions—in the area, due to climate change, which he noticed in the mid 1990s. As Barbera has higher acidity than Neb-

Franesco Versio, winemaker, Bruno Giacosa.

biolo, Gaja implemented this change to create a better balanced wines. (Note that he still does produce a Barbaresco from 100% Nebbiolo every vintage.)

Gaja's wines offer tremendous weight on the palate as well as marvelous complexity and of course, ideal structure. They are made in a more modern fashion with barrique aging, so this style varies from the traditionalists of Barbaresco; you may prefer Gaja's wine, you may prefer others. But there is room for both approaches and certainly Angelo Gaja is an significant producer and today remains one of the most important ambassadors of Barbaresco throughout the world.

The Wines and Foods of Piemonte

New challenges face the producers of Barbaresco today; one of these is climate change, which has brought about modifications in the vineyards, according to Francesco Versio, winemaker at Bruno Giacosa. "In the last 10–12 years, we have had some strange vintages," Versio remarks. "We work in general with Nebbiolo grapes with less acidity than in the past." To that end, Versio varies harvest dates in the vineyard as well as maceration times in the cellar to achieve the best balanced wines; for the warm 2011 growing season, for example, Versio notes that they harvested grapes from their Santo Stefano cru on September 19th, far earlier than normal.

Today, quality is at an all-time high in Barbaresco, thanks to visionaries such as Gaja as well as the detailed work of traditionalists such as Vacca. Time does not stand still, so the best producers know that they must be innovators to some degree, whatever their style. Ceretto has been refining his examples of Barbaresco (as well as his Barolo) to produce more pure wines, ones that better reflect his belief in more natural and healthier wines. "My style focuses on reflecting today's characteristics. I think that today's winemakers are pushing and influencing too much the taste of the wines and it is easier to recognize a winemaker (or brand) than it is a terroir," he states.

Bruna Giacosa talks about Barbaresco

Bruna Giacosa is the daughter of Bruno Giacosa, one of Italy's most legendary wine producers; their winery, located in Neive, is one of the most revered in Barbaresco and all of Piemonte (the winery is also well known for its magnificent offerings of Barolo).

How does she see Barbaresco as compared to Barolo? "I think Barbaresco is a great wine," she says. "But it's not as well known as Barolo, for example. Barbaresco can age like Barolo and when you drink a great Barbaresco, you have great emotion, because you find a lot of finesse, a lot of elegance."

"In the future, I hope people will understand that Barbaresco is as good as Barolo. The only difference for me is that Barbaresco is a little more feminine and Barolo is more masculine. I opt for Barbaresco when I like to drink a wine with elegance and finesse. You will find these qualities in some Barolos, but I find it more often in Barbaresco. For me, Barbaresco is on the same level as Barolo."

To that end, Ceretto has changed a good deal of his work in the vineyards and cellar. "I've been working in biodynamic, which means a total respect for the soil." He also is decreasing the use of barrique and working more with botti. "Don't push the tannins (with Nebbiolo), because if you do, you will have problems with the nose. This doesn't happen with botti."

In the Barbaresco production zone, there are more and more producers that are reflecting Ceretto's theme of balance, regardless of a traditional or more modern approach. "It is a path," Ceretto states, "to rediscover the real potential of my wines and my terroirs that, from my point of view, the new technologies were covering up."

FOUR

Roero

Head south from Alba, and soon you will be amongst the eleven communes where Barolo is produced. Head a bit east of Alba and you will find yourself in the land of Barbaresco. Now journey west of Alba, across the Tanaro River, and you will discover the Roero district, home of some beautifully structured wines, also made from the Nebbiolo variety. Yet, while Barolo and Barbaresco are celebrated for their complexity and longevity, the red wines of Roero are too often ignored.

In the chapter on white wines later in this book, I will discuss the excellent versions of Roero Arneis that are produced in this zone. But as popular as those wines have become over the past few decades, the wines here from Nebbiolo, labeled simply as Roero, have not earned a great deal of popularity. Perhaps the fact that the label doesn't refer to the Nebbiolo grape is a problem, but it's more basic than that. For many consumers and wine buyers, Roero is about the white wines, not the reds.

The reality in Roero is that the red wines are very good to excellent in quality, with the best versions offering the depth of fruit and structure to warrant aging for 10–20 years from the finest vintages. But the wines in general are lighter than those of Barolo and Barbaresco, due to several particulars, most importantly, soil. The Roero district is largely comprised of sandy soils, which often

Carlo Deltetto, Deltetto.

results in red wines of marvelous fragrances, but without the tannic structure of the most powerful reds.

Carlo Deltetto, of the eponymous winery in Canale, explains. "The terroir is soft and permeable, made from sandstone, sedimentary rocks of marine origin comprised of limestone, clay and sand." Comparing Roero's earth with that of the Langhe, he notes that across the river, the Langhe's hills are older, with "the soil being more compact . . . dominated by white and grey marl, sedimentary rocks of marine origin made of limestone and clay." For Deltetto, this soil gives wines that are "elegant, but in general more structured." He notes this is particularly true for Barolo,

The Wines and Foods of Piemonte

while he believes that the wines of Barbaresco, being a bit lighter than Barolo, are more similar to Roero.

As the Roero reds are not as well structured as their more famous counterparts from the Langhe, aging requirements are less; six months in wood is the minimum for both Roero Rosso and *riserva;* contrast this with one year for Barbaresco and eighteen months for Barolo.

Among the best examples of Roero are the "Torretta" bottling from Marco Porello, which offers precise acidity and elegant tannins; the "Sudisfà" (classic bottling and the *riserva*) from Angelo Negro; the "Braja" *riserva* from Deltetto, the "Pasiunà" from Enrico Serafino, with distinctive dark cherry and incense notes, the "Rocche D'Ampsej" *riserva* from Matteo Coreggia (particularly distinguished) and the "Renesio" and "Mombeltrano" *riserve* from Malvirà. At a visit to this excellent producer in the fall of 2015, I was able to taste several older offerings of their Roero, including a 1996 *superiore*, which displayed tar, dark cherry and cedar notes, while promising some seven to ten tears of life ahead of it—yes, Roero can age quite well, indeed.

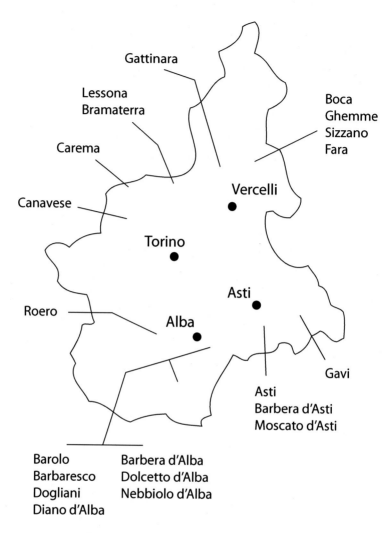

Gattinara

Lessona
Bramaterra

Boca
Ghemme
Sizzano
Fara

Carema

Vercelli

Canavese

Torino

Roero

Asti

Alba

Gavi

Asti
Barbera d'Asti
Moscato d'Asti

Barolo
Barbaresco
Dogliani
Diano d'Alba

Barbera d'Alba
Dolcetto d'Alba
Nebbiolo d'Alba

Major wine production zones and their wine types.
©Alessandro Masnaghetti.

The Wines and Foods of Piemonte

FIVE

Alto Piemonte Reds

Piemonte is much more than the celebrated reds of the Langhe or Monferrato. Alto Piemonte is an expansive territory filled with little pockets of vineyards that are the source for some of the most unheralded red wines in Italy.

Alto Piemonte incorporates such distinctive production zones as Gattinara, Boca, Bramaterra and Lessona, each quite small and each with red wines based on the Nebbiolo variety. This may be the same grape as planted in Barolo and Barbaresco, but the wines here are very different in style; some of this can be explained with the varietal regulations, as the last three wines mentioned can contain varying percentages of grapes such as Vespolina and Uva Rara.

Yet one has to look at factors such as soil and climate to understand why these Nebbiolo-based wines are so unique, as Martina Fogerty of Vallana winery in the town of Maggiora in Novara province, not far from Lago Maggiore and the border with Lombardia, explains. "Alto Piemonte is on the borderline between Mediterranean and continental climate, while the Langhe is warmer and dryer," Fogerty notes. "Also, even though the average temperature in a year can be very close, we have a greater day/night excursion due to the influence of cold currents that come down from the nearby Alps."

Vineyards of Travaglini, Gattinara.

The Wines and Foods of Piemonte

This generally translates into long, cool growing seasons, although recent trends in climate change have meant earlier harvests, as elsewhere in Piemonte. Still these wines quite often display slightly higher levels of acidity than their counterparts from the Langhe, so there is excellent aging potential for Alto Piemonte reds.

One of the most celebrated estates in Alto Piemonte is Le Piane, owned by Christoph Kunzli, a Swiss native. Working in the wine business in his homeland afforded him numerous trips to Italy and he soon started to learn about winemaking. He was charmed by many Italian reds, especially those from the Campo dei Piane estate of Antonio Cerri. This was situated in the Boca DOC, not far from the town of Maggiora and Lago d'Orto, situated north of Vercelli and slightly northwest of Novara. Kunzli loved the structure and Burgundian style of these wines, produced primarily from Nebbiolo and Vespolina. He eventually purchased the property when Cerri became too ill to tend the vineyards; he has been producing several red wines here since the late 1990s.

His top wine is Boca, an area that is a shadow of its former self. Kunzli points out that there were once 40,000 hectares of vines planted in Alto Piemonte as recently as the 1930s (this is a larger total than all of Tuscany today), but currently that number has shrunk to less than one-tenth of that amount (today, there are fewer than ten producers of Boca).

Thus he has bucked the trend of people moving away from viticulture in this area (it simply became too expensive for most vintners to produce wine here); he makes approximately 40,000 bottles per year, with Boca representing about half of his production. The wine, aged solely in *botti grandi*-"the style of my wine was always clear-big barrels, long aging," he remarks—is unmistakable in its Nebbiolo aromatic profile, but with the acidity of the Vespolina, this has a more elegant, more refined feel in its youth than most examples of other great Nebbiolo, such as Barolo and Barbaresco. The tannins are especially graceful and there is marvelous complexity and outstanding balance, especially in recent vintages such as 2006, 2008 (the latter, arguably his best effort as of this writing in 2016) and 2010; look for these wines to drink well for anywhere from 10–15 years, perhaps longer.

Perhaps the main reason for the success of the Le Piane Boca is that Kunzli always makes a wine that reflects balance and not power. "Boca is a wine built upon acidity and not tannins. You're never sure with tannins, as they dry out. But you're always sure with acidity, as it preserves freshness." Given this philosophy, Boca has a strong future ahead of it. (Incidentally, his other red wines are quite stylish, especially the "Maggiorina" offering, a lighter version, if you will, of Boca, while his "Piane", with as much as 90% Croatina, is a more rustic red with sumptuous aromas of black plum, marmalade and oregano.)

Gattinara

While Boca has always been relatively unknown, Gattinara has become much more famous, as this is the arguably today the best-known Alto Piemonte red. Much of the reason for this is the Travaglini family, who owns a total of 60 of the production zone's 100 hectares. Gattinara is required to be produced exclusively from Nebbiolo; the Travaglini vineyards are situated between 320–420 meters (1050 to 1360 feet) above sea level; at this elevation, the grapes ripen slowly, giving the wines good natural acidity and structure.

Cinzia Travaglini and her husband Massimo Collauto produce several examples of Gattinara, each aged in Slavonian oak *botti*. The classic Gattinara rests two years in these casks, followed by eight months in bottle, while the *riserva* spends three years in wood with eight months of bottle aging. The classic offering displays youthful tannins, very good acidity (especially in years such as 2004 and 2008) and firm, but balanced tannins; aromas such as strawberry, dried cherry and sage are present. Medium-full, with very good richness on the palate.

The *riserva* takes things up a notch or two with layers of fruit that coat the mouth, while the tannins are a bit stronger. The practice of traditional winemaking, as with the aging in large casks,

Vineyards of Le Piane, Boca.

allows not only the local terroir to emerge, but also the vintage
differences. The aromas are more pronounced along floral lines
(orange and red roses along with notes of cedar and sage), while
the wine is generally made from slightly riper grapes, yet still offering very good acidity. Tasted side by side at the winery in 2014,
the 2007 *riserva* is very rich with great Nebbiolo purity, while the
2008 is silkier with more finesse and slightly higher acid levels.
Both wines have excellent to outstanding complexity with elegant
tannins (even quite velvety in the 2008). Both wines will age well,
with the 2008 offering the promise of 15–20 years of drinking
pleasure, although given the history of this wine, that estimate
may be a bit conservative, as this is one of the finest efforts by
Travaglini to date.

Clearly, Gattinara at its finest is the equal of Barolo and Barbaresco. "Yes, Gattinara has a long life," says Cinzia Travaglini. We
recently opened a magnum of 1967 Gattinara and it showed great
freshness and plenty of life—it was a beautiful experience." Other impressive Gattinara preoducers include Nervi—look for their
"Molsino" bottling, produced from ideally situated vineyards—

Massimo Collauto, Travaglini.

and Antoniolo, whose "San Francesco" offering is aged in both mid-sized tonneaux as well as *botti grandi*.

Ghemme

A few miles east of Gattinara, situated across the Sésia River, is the Ghemme production zone. Quite small—there are only 50 to 60 hectares (125 to 150 acres) planted in this zone—most of the vineyards are situated about 250 to 300 meters (820 to 984 feet above sea level).

The leading estate here is Cantalupo—formally known as

Antichi Vigneti di Cantalupo—manged today by Alberto Arlunno. A warm, passionate man, he has an encyclopedic knowledge of this small area, explaining that this land is the result of plate tectonics, when the African plate crashed with Europe, forming a "super" volcano. He notes that while nearby Gattinara is characterized by magma that became solid and created stones in that soil, in Ghemme, these same stones do not exist. "The particular stone we find here in Ghemme," Arlunno notes, "is limestone," while these soils are also comprised of porphyr, quartz and granite.

Arlunno's family began growing grapes in the 1800s; his first year of production under the Cantalupo label was 1977 (Ghemme became a DOC in 1969 and was later recognized as a DOCG in 1997). His examples of Ghemme are always 100% Nebbiolo, although the regulations allow for 15% of local varieties such as Uva Rara or Vespolina. Among his Ghemme wines are "Anno Primo", meant for consumption within five to seven years of the vintage date, as well as three longer-lived wines: "Collis Carellae," "Collis Breclamae" and "Signore di Bayand"; these wines are at their best at seven to ten years of age, although the finest vintages can be aged for twelve to fifteen years. Aged solely in *grandi botti* (some as large as 80 hl!)these wines are rustic, with aromas of tobacco and cum-

Lessona, Bramaterra and Other Alto Piemonte Reds

Lessona and Bramaterra, primarily Nebbiolo blended with Vespolina and/or Croatina, are two other noteworthy Alto Piemonte reds. Though the zones are close, there are some differences, according to Cristiano Garella, winemaker at La Prevostura (Lessona) and Le Pianelle (Bramaterra). "Lessona has a marina sandy soil with an acidic pH, so the wines are more floral, very aromatic with soft tannins," Garella remarks. "Bramaterra in general has a porphyric soil with an acidic pH, very rich in iron and potassium, so the wines are more mineral-driven with more fruit and tannins than Lessona."

I'll briefly mention Fara and Sizzano, two other local Nebbiolo-based reds as well; there are only a few producers of these wines, with the Boniperti "Barton", a 70% Nebbiolo/30% Vespolina, being one of the most elegant, traditionally made examples of Fara. You will have more success finding reds under the Coste della Sesia and Colline Novaresi designations; the former encompasses the Gattinara production zone and several other local villages, while the latter is a secondary appellation for Ghemme, Boca, Fara and Sizzano.

What's admirable about these wines is the fact that most examples are fine values, especially those labeled for a variety, be it Nebbiolo, Vespolina or Croatina. These are medium-bodied offerings meant for consumption within the first three to five years, as they have mid-weight tannins.

Look for examples such as the Tiziano Mazzoni Nebbiolo del Monteregio, Francesca Castaldi Vespolina "Nina" (both Colline Novaresi DOC) as well as the Travaglini Nebbiolo and the Tenute Sella "Orbello," a blend of five red grapes (both Coste delle Sesia DOC). If you are a fan of rosé, there are a few fabulous Coste della Sesia rosati, especially the Sperino "Rosa di Rosa," the Le Pianelle "Al Posto dei Fiori" and the La Prevostura "Corrina," this last one of Italy's finest rosés. Cristiano Garella, the winemaker of these last two wines, believes Nebbiolo is an ideal variety for the production of rosé, due to its pale color as well as its "variety of aromas, such as cinnamon, pomegranate and bitter orange." Very dry with great character, these can stand up to hearty local pastas or even lighter game.

in as well as dried cherry fruit, and take their time to display their best qualities; in a visit to the winery in 2014, I tasted the 2005 bottlings of the "Breclamae" and "Signore." I was especialy impressed with the weight of the former, as 2005 was not a particularly rich year anywhere in Piemonte; the acidity was quite good and the tannins were very elegant.

These are wines for traditional Nebbiolo lovers, those who appreciate varietal focus and a sense of place just as much as (or more than) complexity and ageworthiness. "After coming here and tasting Ghemme and other wines of this region," notes Arlunno," I'm more convinced now that we can make a luxury wine, the highest rated wine. Here I found a wine of great bouquet."

Other examples of noteworthy Ghemme include those from Tiziano Mazzoni (both the classic "dei Mazzoni" version and the especially lovely "Ai Livelli"), Monsecco and the Francesco Brigatti Ghemme "Oltre il Bosco," a traditionally-made classic.

SIX

Carema and Ossola Valley

While there are several DOC zones north and west of Alto Piemonte that produce distinct reds, I will briefly deal in this chapter with only two: Carema and the Ossola Valley, given their uniqueness.

Carema is named for the town at the border of the Piemonte and Valle d'Aosta regions; the production zone is located entirely within the Canavese D.O.C. territory. While the wines must contain a minimum of 85% Nebbiolo, almost every version—there are only a handful of producers—is Nebbiolo *in purezza*. The most unique feature about this small zone are the terraced vineyards, which have overhead canopies that are supported by concrete pylons (*piloni*). Vines sit on top of large rocks, which absorb the sun's heat during the day and then release it at night, thus maintaining an ideal temperature variation during the growing season.

There are two major producers of Carema: Ferrando and the Cantina Produttori di Carema, a cooperative producer with about 75 grower members. Each has a classic version as well as a *riserva*; the black label classic offering from the Produttori is a sensual wine with notes of dried cherry, red pepper flakes and a hint of tobacco. Offering an elegant entry on the palate along with precise acidity (especially in the 2012 version), this has beautiful varietal focus (it is 100% Nebbiolo), outstanding complexity as well as lovely charm and finesse; this is a feminine version of Nebbiolo. It is also one of Piemonte's (and perhaps all of Italy's) greatest red wine values.

The Ferrando "Etichetta Nera" (black label) is a richer, riper, more modern style of Carema, as it is matured for at least two years in barriques (as opposed to the Produttori wine, aged in large oak casks). Produced only in exceptional vintages—and limited to about 3000 bottles at that—this offers impressive weight on the palate and demands at least seven years after release before it displays its best qualities, although the wine is even better after a decade; it is one of the finest examples of Nebbiolo in all of Piemonte.

Ossola Valley

In far northeastern Piemonte, in the area that borders with Switzerland, the Ossola Valley is a wine growing area that reminds one of long ago. Here Cantine Garrone, managed by Mario Garrone, produces red and white wines (primarily the former) from grapes tended by the local growers' association.

As one might imagine, the winters are harsh, but spring and summer welcome in moderate temperatures and cool nights, ideal for well structured wines. An ancient glacier once stood where vineyards are now situated; soils are comprised of sand and pebbles (which aides drainage) as well as small amounts of clay. Vines are planted on terraced hillsides, traditionally grown using a pergola training system known locally as Toppia that is supported by stone columns; this limits yields, resulting in more concentrated wines.

The principal grape is Prünent, a mutation of Nebbiolo, that has adapted to the local terroir. Garrone notes that Prünent has a typical Nebbiolo color, but that in general, "it has less concentration that a Nebbiolo-based wine of southern Piemonte, while there is more pronounced acidity. We are always happy with the complexity of the aromatics; our wines made from Prünent are an ideal mix of structure, elegance and finesse."

Garrone produces two reds that incorporate Prünent: Cà d'Maté, which has 10% of this variety to go along with 70% Nebbiolo and 20% Croatina; the other offering is the Prünent, exclusively from this variety, which interestingly is labeled as Valli Ossolane DOC Nebbiolo Superiore. This wine is made from older vines, some them being pre-phylloxera, while the Cà d'Maté has a small percentage of younger vines. The Prünent is matured in 50% new oak barrels for one year and then aged in bottle for an additional year before sale. Garrone believes this wine has "great aging potential," recalling a few examples that were in fine shape at fifteen years of age.

SEVEN

Barbera

As Piemonte's most widely planted red variety, Barbera is at once treasured and at the same time, thought of in less than stellar terms. It's consumed on a daily basis at the family table and in *osterie* and *trattorie* throughout the region and that's something that will probably never change. But it's also been elevated by some producers to a level of a "serious" wine, one that has been given a new level of respect by the wine media, ever hungry for riper and more robust red wines.

If we view Barbera from the simple terms of a red wine meant for food, it is a great success. "There is no other red wine that is as important with food as Barbera," says Luca Currado, who produces several notable versions at Vietti in Castiglione Falleto. Perhaps the most important reasons for this are the grape's high levels of natural acidity as well as low to moderate tannins. This high acidity is perfect at lunch when one needs a red to pair with local *salumi*, as the acidity cuts right through the fat of the meat. Also, given the lightness of tannins-the wine doesn't need to be laid aside for several years—it's drinkable upon release.

This has been the tradition of Barbera throughout Piemonte for decades and it continues today with examples from cooperative producers such as Vinchio-Veglio Serra and Cantina di Nizza as well as great family producers such as Vietti and Michele

Massimo Pastura, Cascina La Ghersa.

Chiarlo, with their Barbera "Tre Vigne" and Barbera "Le Orme" bottlings, respectively (both firms also produce more powerful examples of Barbera as well).

Yet in the 1970s, a few producers in the province of Asti were convinced they could make a Barbera that could be something much more than just a simple, easy-to-drink red. They wanted to create a new identity for Barbera, making it a much more complex and ageworthy wine that wine journalists and the public would take more seriously. The late Giacomo Bologna was at the forefront of this movement, one that continues today, with the evolution of the Nizza subzone in Asti, where some of the most powerful examples of Barbera are crafted.

The three most famous examples of Barbera are Barbera d'Alba, Barbera d'Asti and Barbera Monferrato. The first examples are from vineyards near Alba in the province of Cuneo, the second from Asti province to the east and the third in southeastern Piemonte that encompasses parts of the provinces of Asti and Alessandria to the immediate east.

I will begin with a comparison of Barbera d'Alba and Barbera d'Asti and will follow up with a few thoughts on Barbera Monferrato. An important difference to note here is that Barbera d'Alba is made by producers that often make Barolo or Barbaresco; as these two wines are much more famous and renowned, it is clear that the best vineyards in these zones are reserved for Nebbiolo, meaning Barbera is relegated to secondary sites. This does not mean vineyards of poor quality, rather just not the best (in most instances).

Barbera d'Asti is a different story however, as the finest sites are indeed planted to Barbera, since Nebbiolo is not a principal grape of this province. Thus it is relatively safe to say that Barbera d'Asti will generally be more powerful and complex than the examples from Alba and numerous producers in the area have taken steps to bring about an identity of intensity and ageworthiness for Asti Barbera.

One of those producers is Massimo Pastura of Cascina La Ghersa in the small hamlet of Moasca. Pastura is a quietly engaging man who wins you over with his charm and direct, honest manner; it should come as no surprise that his wines reflect his personality. "Working the correct way with low yields, proper selection of the grapes and very careful fermentations, we can make examples of Barbera of the same quality level as the premium wines of Italy, such as Brunello and Barolo," he proudly remarks.

Pastura produces as many as four different examples of Barbera d'Asti; for comparison sake, his "Piagè" and "Vignassa" versions are model examples of his style, offering texture and grace. The former is aged solely in steel tanks and sees no wood; displaying red plum, lavender and cedar aromas and a rich mid-palate, this is a beautifully balanced wine with great Barbera purity that is a pleasure to drink. The latter, from a very old vineyard in the Nizza zone, is aged in barriques, but the wood notes do not overwhelm the beautiful aromatics of black raspberry and violets. This is quite rich with a lengthy finish and excellent acidity that along with the depth of fruit, ensures great aging potential. The 2010, tasted in mid-2014 has at least another five to seven years of life ahead of it, while the 1998 (a very underrated year), tasted at the same time, still displays remarkable freshness and should be at peak sometime around 2018 or 2019.

While the La Ghersa wines are models of restraint, numerous producers in Asti, especially those who produce Barbera from the Nizza sub-zone, make very forceful offerings, wines that certainly impress with their deep color and super ripe fruit, yet push the boundaries as far as balance and terroir. Often these wines are aged in barriques for two years and display a great deal of spice from the oak; combine that with smaller yields, which increases the tannins and you have wines that are powerful and can be slightly out of control. Purchasing Barbera d'Asti is clearly a case of *caveat emptor*.

The various examples of Barbera d'Asti from Tenuta Garetto in Agliano Terme are evidence of the stylistic distinctions of local Barbera; winemaker Alessandro Garetto crafts three very different versions of this wine, based on how the wine is aged. The first example, "*Tra Neuit e Dì*" ("between night and day" in local dialect), is an old-fashioned approach to Barbera, as this wine is aged solely in steel tanks. The second version known as "*In Pectore*," is made in an approach between traditional and contemporary, as it has been partially matured in barriques, while the third wine "Favà," is an unabashedly modern approach to Barbera, as it is aged for 12–14 months in French barriques, almost totally new. Very deep in color with aromas of black plum, black raspberry, clove, tar and

Alessandro Garetto produces deeply concentrated
Barbera d'Asti at his estate in Agliano Terme.

vanilla, the wine is quite impressive in terms of richness and persistence, while there are ample notes of oak. While I have found
a few vintages in the past to be a bit oaky in their approach, the
recently released 2012 offers a much better equilibrium between
fruit and wood; this is the finest example of this wine I have tasted
to date; it will pair well with roast fowl and lighter game. Incidentally, while the "Favà" has brought great acclaim to Garetto, I must
admit to loving the simple charms of his "*Tra Neuit e Dì*" offering,
especially paired with *coniglio brasato* (braised rabbit).

Other firms that also make various styles of Barbera d'Asti include Pico Maccario and Bersano. The former is a small winery operated by two brothers who have a similar approach in the cellar as Garetto; ranging from the steel-aged "Lavignone" to the "Tre Roveri" offering, matured in various-sized casks, from *tonneaux* to *botti* and finally "Epico," which is aged solely in barrique.

At Bersano, an historic, highly respected estate founded in 1907, there are also various style of Barbera d'Asti including a very modern example from Nizza. Yet it is their "Costalunga" offering aged in large Slavonian oak casks that might just be their best wine; it is certainly their most traditional. It's a particular favorite of mine, as it reminds me of how Barbera d'Asti used to taste back in the 1960s and '70s, before the small oak barrels came along; here is a wine that is elegant with unmatched varietal purity and charm; even better, it's simply delicious!

Earlier I mentioned the name of Giacomo Bologna as being at the forefront of the movement to elevate Barbera d'Asti to new heights; he started this in the early 1980s with a Barbera from the Bricco dell'Uccellone vineyard near his estate in Rocchetta Tanaro. Here was a truly unique wine, a Barbera aged in small wooden barrels that displayed the spice and very ripe fruit akin to some of the most celebrated red wines of the world. It certainly shook up the Barbera world, especially as many other producers in the Asti zone, noticing the media attention for this wine, emulated Bologna's approach and began to craft their own more modern, "important" examples of Barbera.

Raffaella Bologna, Giacomo's daughter, who along with her brother Giuseppe, has been at the helm of the family estate, known as Braida, since her father's death in 1990, recalls that this approach was a bit divisive at the time. "The feeling at the time from winemakers around Italy was controversial," she recalls. "Italy was split 50% between traditionalist versus revolutionary." She remembers that some individuals tasting this wine called it a "Barbera Barololeggia" for its resemblance to Barolo; others thought her father was blending other grapes in the wine.

Today that controversy is nothing more than a fleeting historical moment, as Bricco dell'Uccellone is today regarded as one of Italy's finest wines. Medium-full with excellent depth of fruit and persistence, there is an impressive array of flavors such as blackberry, tar, clove and tobacco that are beautifully meshed together; the oak is evident, but ideally integrated. Aproachable upon release, this is a wine that improves with time, with the finest vintages displaying their full potential from age seven to ten years.

Given that so many other producers in Asti have been influenced by this wine as well as Bricco della Bigotta, a similarly-styled single vineyard Barbera that Bologna introduced only three years after Uccellone, you could say that these revolutionary wines from Bologna are today considered standard bearers. What was once an uncertain trail is now a busy thoroughfare!

Bologna continued to push boundaries with Barbera, especially with "Ai Suma", a late harvest offering produced in only the best years. Today this is the wine that is, at least to me, a controversial selection, a bit extreme in its super ripe style, yet one cannot deny its impressive depth of fruit. Like it or not, this wine was another chapter of Giacomo Bologna's philosophy of creating new boundaries. His daugher Raffaella beautifully sums up this man's true value with these words; "He gave producers the courage to leave behind the path of tradition and to cross new roads."

Barbera d'Alba

Regarding Barbera d'Alba, while it does not get the attention of its counterpart from Asti, realize that dozens of Barolo and Barbaresco producers regularly turn out noteworthy examples that offer excellent complexity and impressive varietal character. Among my favorites are the E. Mirafiore; Elio Grasso "Vigna Martina;" Ca' Viola "Bric de Luv;" Fontanafredda "Raimonda;" and Roberto Voerzio "Vigna Pozzo dell'Annunziata" Riserva, a wine this producer bottles only in magnums.

The firm of Pio Cesare in Alba produces a classic Barbera d'Alba as well as a cru offering named Fides (Latin for "faith"). Matured

Scarrone Vineyard, Castiglione Falletto, source of one of the greatest examples of old vine Barbera.

Barbera lovers often seek out the ripest, most expressive versions of this variety; their search often leads them to Barbera from the Nizza zone in Asti. Named for the town of Nizza Monferrato, the zone encompasses eighteen different villages, including San Marzano Oliveto and Moasca in the south (just a few kilometers west of Nizza Monferrato) to Incisa Scappino at the eastern limits to Agliano Terme, Vinchio and Mombercelli farther north.

Barberas from this zone have been identified as Barbera d'Asti Superiore Nizza (DOCG) for years, but as of the 2014 vintage, the wines can be identified as Nizza Superiore, as long as the disciplinare regulations are met. This includes vineyards that are south facing as well those farmed to reduced yields. For his Favà Barbera from the Nizza zone (the vineyard is in Agliano Terme), Alessandro Garetto comments that he works "with 4 to 4.5 tons per hectare," with the maximum yield for Nizza Barbera is 7.5 tons.

What makes this zone so special for Barbera and what are the characteristics of these wines? "It's a combination of elevation and soil," says Ignazio Giovine of L'Armangia in Canelli. This town is known for Moscato, not Barbera, so Giovine sources his Barbera from vineyards in the Nizza zone. "The Nizza valley is just two or three kilometers north, but the climate and soils are completely different," he remarks. "There is more clay and limestone in the soil, while Canelli is more sand. The climate in Nizza is warmer and drier, which is better for Barbera."

in a combination of small and large oak, this latter wine offers inviting aromas of red cherry, red plum and tar and is beautifully structured; the oak notes are subdued and there is very good acidity along with distinctive spice. This is one of this firm's most intriguing wines and one of the signature examples of Barbera d'Alba.

Arguably the most famous examples of Barbera d'Alba are those of Vietti at the Scarrone vineyard near the winery in Castiglione Falletto. There are two versions, with the "Vigna Vecchia" ("old vine") bottling from a part of the vineyard planted in 1918. Both wines are labeled as Scarrone and display beautiful black plum and black raspberry flavors with the "Vigna Vecchia" almost decadent in its ripeness and explosion of fruit on the palate. Given the age of the vines, yields are very small, resulting in a deeply concentrated wine. The Scarrone "Vigna Vecchia" is absolutely delicious upon release and can be enjoyed for at least seven to ten years after release.

Luca Currado, winemaker at Vietti, has noted the recent interest in Barbera in both Alba and Asti, but realizes that it was not always this way. "You have to think that we (producers and growers in general) considered Barbera as a secondary grape in the Barolo zone. But this is a huge error." He comments that there used to be a lot of vineyards within the Barolo region planted to Barbera, but that "in the early 1900s, many of these plantings were ripped out in favor of Nebbiolo for Barolo."

Having crafted beautiful examples of Barbera d'Alba from the Scarrone cru, Vietti wanted to make more Barbera, so some twenty years ago, his family purchased a wonderful vineyard called La Crena in Agliano d'Asti that was planted in the early to mid 1930s. Currado describes this wine as "powerful, intense, a masculine Barbera, darker in color than from Alba, more inky." As a producer of first-rate examples of Barbera from both Alba and Asti, Currado has a unique perspective on the styles of these wines. "To make it simple, I always say that Asti is the Angelina Jolie of Barbera and Alba is the Grace Kelly of Barbera—it is a wine you want to dance with."

The Barbera d'Alba zone also extends to the Roero district, across the Tanaro river from the city of Alba and surrounding communes. Excellent examples here include the Pelassa "San Pancrazio" Superiore, the "MonBrione" of Monchiero Carbone, the "Parduné" Superiore from Enrico Serafino and the Matteo Coreggia "Marun". This last wine, from a beautifully situated hill 310 meters (1015 feet) above sea level, is one of the mosty stylish Barberas from

Summing up, Giovine explains the key to Nizza Barbera. "Longer life, complexity. The flavor is still alive after 10–12 years. Normally a young Barbera after two to three years loses its flavor. Older wines from Nizza remain young and fresh."

anywhere in the region, with its blackberry and mincemeat flavors backed by a rich mid-palate and excellent concentration.

Barbera del Monferrato

As for Barbera del Monferrato, this is generally a style of Barbera that is restrained as well as traditional, as many producers of this wine make a version that emphasizes the natural high acidity of this grape without a lot of small new oak influence.

Ths production zone encompasses a good part of the Barbera d'Asti zone as well as a small area to the north and east in the province of Alessandria. While most producers release a Barbera *in purezza,* the regulations do allow for 15% of a select few local varieties, such as Freisa, Grignolino or Dolcetto. Generally, the typical Monferrato Barbera is medium-bodied, as producers here aim for a drinkable wine, not one meant for high scores from the media. Notable examples of Barbera Monferrato include versions from producers such as Gaudio Bricco Mondalino, Iuli ("Barbabba" and "Umberta"), Luigi Tacchino, Villa Sparina (a noted Gavi producer) and Accornero ("Bricco Batista" and "Giulin").

Other Barbera

Barbera is planted in many zones throughout Piemonte and is treated in so many fashions. In Gavi, which is part of the Barbera Monferrato zone, Massimiliana Spinola of Castello di Tassarolo produces a stunning Barbera called "Titouan" named for one of the heavy horses used for plowing the vineyards at this biodynamic estate. Designated as Piemonte DOC, this is a voluptuous Barbera with deep purple color, marvelous ripeness and amazing varietal focus. Fermented and aged solely in steel tanks and made without the addition of sulphites, this is pure Barbera at its most tantalizing and appealing. The 2013, tasted at the winery in the fall of 2014, was superb; immediately drinkable, it should peak in another five to seven years.

At Vigne Marina Coppi, situated in the Colli Tortonesi hills near the hamlet of Castellania in Alessandra province, winemaker/co-proprietor Francesco Bellocchio produces several offerings of Barbera. Sourced from estate plantings at an elevation of 400 meters (1300 feet), the bluish/gray clay, limestone and sand soils of these vineyards, known as Sant'Agata (named for a nearby town) are ideal for this variety, lending notable finesse to these Barberas. The "Sant'Andrea" version, blended with 15% Croatina, is aged solely in steel tanks and offers enticing floral perfumes and is quite delicious, while the "I Grop" Superiore named for the eponymous cru with 40–50 year old vines, is 100% Barbera aged in *botti*. Displaying black plum and lavender aromas along with hints of chocolate and a pleasant dustiness, this has big extract, excellent persistence, bright fruit and lively acidity (especially in the 2010 version), and is a Barbera of beautiful complexity that will appeal for some five to seven years.

EIGHT

Dolcetto

Dolcetto is one of the most delicious, most agreeable and most distinctive wines of Piemonte. It's also a wonderful accompaniment to numerous local foods, ranging from lighter pastas and prosciutto to young cheeses such as Toma or Robiola di Roccaverano as well as poultry or pork.

Yet it never receives the attention it deserves, no doubt due to the simple fact that it's not Nebbiolo. That variety produces wines that can age for decades, while the Dolcetto grape is made into offerings that are generally meant for consumption upon release and for another three to five years after that. If you believe that bigger is better, than Dolcetto may not overwhelm you. But if you value varietal purity along with finesse and charm in a red wine, then you'll appreciate Dolcetto. I know I do; in fact, I have a thirty year-plus love affair with Dolcetto and I always look forward to tasting as many examples as I can when I'm in Piemonte.

Dolcetto is planted in many zones in the region; there are eight different D.O.C. zones, which is a blessing and a curse. Certainly there are successful versions produced in various areas, but having so many appellations can only cause confusion. This situation is one reason why Dolcetto is not as much in demand as it should be, but the primary reason is even more basic. It's the name of the grape that's at the crux of the matter, as Dolcetto liter-

Countryside at Valdibà, Dogliani production zone.

ally means "little sweet one." A red wine that's sweet? Who would want that?

Of course, Dolcetto is not a sweet red wine, but a pleasing dry one, sometimes with fairly serious tannins found in the best-structured examples. The "sweet" suggestion refers to the ripe fruit in this variety, as a young Dolcetto bursts forth with zesty notes of black raspberry, cranberry and black plum that make it instantly appealing, both on the nose and palate. Most producers want to emphasize the fruit-driven character of Dolcetto, so aging takes place in stainless steel tanks or cement vats, so as not to take away from the simple delights of this wine.

Getting back to the various zones in which Dolcetto is planted, there are four that stand out: Dolcetto d'Alba, from areas where Barolo and Barbaresco are produced; Dolcetto di Diano d'Alba, from the small eponymous hillside town in the Barolo zone, Dolcetto di Ovada, from the province of Alessandria, and Dolcetto di Dogliani, from the commune a bit south of the town of Barolo.

Dogliani has become the most famous zone for Dolcetto for several reasons. First, this is the dominant variety planted here, as opposed to the Dolcetto d'Alba zone, where the grape takes a back seat to Nebbiolo or as with Dolcetto d'Asti, where Barbera is much more important.

Secondly, Dogliani has become the zone for the most full-bodied examples of Dolcetto, as the best wines here have the aging potential of a decade or even more, as opposed to the three to five year window for most Dolcettos. Why has this small commune become so successful with Dolcetto?

Nicoletta Bocca, proprietor of the San Fereolo estate in the Valdibà subzone of Dogliani, explains. "We are the perfect place for Dolcetto because the climate needs to be very well balanced. Dolcetto doesn't like excessive heat or cold. Here in the summer, we are open to the mountains (her vineyards are 400–500 meters above sea level), so we can take advantage of fresh breezes." She compares this with the Nebbiolo grape; "Nebbiolo really loves places that can be hot in the summer, but it doesn't like wind."

Dolcetto has been planted in Dogliani for centuries—Bocca notes a document from 1593 that mentioned the grape in this area for the first time. Today there are dozens of beautifully situated hillside vineyards as high as 600 meters above sea level in this zone, several of which are more than 50 or 60 years old. Anna Maria Abbona, at her winery in Moncucco, a small *frazione* just south of Farigliano, one the principal towns of the production zone, makes versions of Dogliani—Sorì di But and Maioli—that are sourced from old vines; the former being a blend of vineyards that have an average age of 40–50 years, while the latter is a cru that was planted in 1936. Abbona notes how tiny the berries are from this vineyard and how small the yields are; needless to say, the Maioli Dogliani (this carries the Superiore designation, meaning it was aged longer at the winery prior to release) from Anna Maria Abbona is a deeply concentrated wine that she recommends consuming six to eight years after the vintage date.

Given how complex and how muscular Dolcetto can be from

Dogliani, it should come as no surprise that the local producers have emphasized the area name. A few years ago the producers agreed to call their best wines simply Dogliani; these would have the D.O.C.G. designation, while wines that did not conform to those rules would still be known as Dolcetto di Dogliani. Certainly having the name of Dogliani on the bottle is a source of pride for these vintners; it would also be synonymous with some of the best wines of Italy and the world. Just as Barolo on a label tells you the wine is Nebbiolo *in purezza,* so too the term Dogliani would now mean a wine made exclusively from Dolcetto within this production zone.

But there was another more basic reason for this change, according to Abbona. "People know Dolcetto as an easy, fruity wine, but here in Dogliani with many very old vineyards and a particular climate we make a very strong and very complex wine.

"So having the name Dolcetto became somewhat of a problem. Thus we decided to just call our best wines Dogliani, meaning that when you see this name, you won't have a prejudice against the wine as you might if it said 'Dolcetto.'"

There are several producers of Dolcetto di Dogliani and Dogliani that regularly craft sumptuous wines. Among the finest is the "San Luigi" offering from Chionetti, a wine that offers delicious juicy cranberry and black raspberry fruit and a sleek finish; this is a wine that is instantly appealing no more than six months after the harvest.

The Luigi Einaudi "Vigna Tecc" Dogliani Superiore is medium-full with excellent complexity, medium-weight tannins and notes of balsamic and dried herbs; this is at its best at five to seven years of age. The "Papà Celso" Dogliani from Marziano Abbona, sourced from 50 plus year-old vines, is almost decadent with its explosive black fruit and hints of pepper in the aromas; aged solely in stainless steel, this is a delight at three to five years of age.

Along with the other two Anna Maria Abbona wines mentioned earlier, this stalwart producer also releases the "San Bernardo" Dogliani Superiore from a vineyard planted in 1943. This is matured for twenty-four months in large casks (25 hectoliters or 2500 liters), unlike her other examples of Dogliani that are aged in stainless steel. Remarkably complex—my comments on the 2009 offering tasted in 2013, noted perfumes of raspberry, plum, red roses and violets—this has very good acidity, medium-weight tannins and excellent persistence; this 2009 San Bernardo, like the best vintages of this wine, should peak at seven to eight years.

One of the reference points for Dogliani is the "Bricco Botti" Superiore offering from Pecchenino. From the winery estate vineyard and aged for two years in 25hl casks, this has the deep fruitiness of Dolcetto backed by a layered mid-palate and an extremely long, harmonious finish. Pecchenino's two other Dogliani, "San Luigi" and Sirì d'Jermu" (the former only steel aged, the latter matured in large casks for one year) are also first-rate, but the "Bricco Botti" offers greater richness along with additional breeding and class. If Dogliani used the Grand Cru system of rating its best sites, this would be at or near the top of the list.

Finally, there are the examples of Dogliani from Bocca at San Fereolo. There is the entry level Dolcetto di Dogliani labeled Valdibà that offers lovely varietal typicity, but it is the San Fereolo bottling, a Dogliani Superiore, that is the star at this estate. This is a wine that has amazing depth of fruit as well as freshness; the 2001, tasted in mid-2014, was a wine from an outstanding vintage that was starting to display secondary aromas, as some of the deep fruit flavors of this wine were starting to tone down a bit. Here is a wine that was almost thirteen years of age, yet would not peak for another five to seven years. Yes, the vines are old and yields are small and oak aging in various cask sizes increases the complexity, but a major ingredient in this wine's identity is the love and care accorded it by Bocca herself.

While Dogliani is home to the most complex, ageworthy examples of Dolcetto, there are some excellent versions from the Dolcetto d'Alba designation. It is true that vintners in this area tend to plant Dolcetto on secondary sites, leaving their best hills

The Wines and Foods of Piemonte

for Nebbiolo. But producers such as Giuseppe Mascarello, Paolo Scavino, Roberto Voerzio, Gianni Voerzio, Rocche Costamagna and Elio Grasso among a few dozen others, do craft excellent examples of Dolcetto, wines that offer beautiful structure and the stuffing to drink well for five to seven years from the finest years.

Another accomplished producer of Dolcetto d'Alba is Marcarini, located in the town of La Morra. Proprietor Manuel Marchetti says that his personal vision for Dolcetto in general is "that it have a good drinkability with good vinous aromas and have the ability to be considered as an everyday wine." He adds that Dolcetto di Dogliani "is more complex in respect to the more drinkable and fruity Dolcetto d'Alba."

Marchetti's opinion on Dolcetto being an everyday wine is widely held, but few would argue that his two cru bottlings of Dolcetto d'Alba at Marcarini are ordinary. The first is from the "Fontanazza" vineyard in La Morra, close to several famous Barolo cru such as Brunate, Cerequio and La Serra. Marchetti speaks of the "magnificent ruby red color with violet reflections" and the "floral and fruit sensations with signs of sweet spices and a delicate, slightly bitter aftertaste."

His second Dolcetto d'Alba is from the "Boschi di Berri" vineyard, also in La Morra. What makes this vineyard special is the fact that the 100 year-old plus vines are on native rootstock and not American, which became necessary when vines throughout Europe were affected in the late 1800s and early 1900s with devastation by phylloxera.

Situated at an elevation of 400 meters (1300 feet), this vineyard produces a Dolcetto with a bouquet of "violets and raspberries" and a "warm and vevelty taste that offers enjoyable sensation of ripe cherries and currants," in Marchetti's words." The structure, harmony and persistence remind us of the traditional late-19th century Dolcetto."

Then we come to Dolcetto di Diano d'Alba, sometimes known simply as Diano d'Alba. This wine is named for the eponymous town, nestled on a hillside in the Barolo production zone

Nicoletta Bocca, San Fereolo, one of Dogliani's
finest producers.

between Grinzane Cavour and Serralunga d'Alba. While there is
a small percentage of Barolo produced from this commune, Dolcetto is the primary variety, as the elevation of the vineyards here
(as high as 500 meters, or 1600 feet above sea level) are ideal for
this grape. The local consorzio has identified the finest vineyards
here; known as *sorì*, which are south-facing and among the highest situated in the commune, there are 77 of these individual sites.

At Fontanafredda in neighboring Serralunga, winemaker

The Wines and Foods of Piemonte

Danilo Drocco produces one of the most famous examples of Dolcetto di Diano d'Alba, known as "La Lepre," named for the wild hare that run through the vineyards. Commenting on Dolcetto from here, Drocco says "the style is unique, because it is a combination of power as in Dogliani, but thanks to the sandy soil, less heavy. Dogliani is full-bodied Dolcetto, while Diano is a rich Dolcetto with great elegance." The "La Lepre" bottling, made from vines of 40 years of age and older, is a bit fuller than a typical Dolcetto di Diano d'Alba; other top producers here include Claudio Alario ("Costa Fiore" and "Montagrillo") and Giovanni Prandi ("Sorì Cristina" and "Sorì Colombè"); consume these charming wines by their fifth birthday.

Finally, a brief mention of Dolcetto di Ovada, produced in the province of Alessandria. Named for the eponymous town, Dolcetto di Ovada (sometimes Dolcetto d'Ovada or simply Ovada) has been overshadowed by the fact this area is part of the Monferrato district, where Barbera is quite famous; the Ovada zone also encompasses a section of the Gavi production zone.

There are about two dozen producers of Dolcetto di Ovada; a few of the top estates are Cascina Boccaccio, Cascina Gentile and Azienda Agricola Luigi Tacchino. Each one of these estates produce two (or more) versions of Dolcetto di Ovada, one aged solely in steel tanks and the other in wood (Boccacio produces two versions aged in wood and also has a wine called "Celso Zero" with no added sulfites.)

Roberto Porciello of Boccacio has vineyards ranging in age from seven to seventy years of age and crafts and ages his wine according to these parameters; fruit from the youngest vines is aged solely in cement tanks for his "Celso" Dolcetto di Ovada. His "é Celso" and his Riserva "Nonno Rucchein" (this a DOCG, labeled simply as Ovada) are matured in barrels ranging from 500 liters (*tonneaux*) for the former and 10 HL *botti* for the latter.

Porciello believes that the high elevation vineyards of Ovada are optimal for structured Dolcetto, one with tannins that are at once velvety, yet have a slightly bitter edge to them with a note of almond. He thinks his 2011 "Nonno Rucchéin", tasted in 2014, has excellent aging potential; when asked how many years, he replies, *"Chi può dirlo? Io scopriremo in futuro!"* ("Who can say? "We'll learn this in the future!"). Incidentally, Porciello recommends that a Dolcetto from Ovada be paired with Ligurian rabbit or with Ovadese *agnolotti* drowned in young Dolcetto from the area—I heartily agree!

NINE

Ruché, Grignolino, Freisa, Pelaverga

The "big three" red varieties of Piemonte, namely Nebbiolo, Dolcetto and Barbera receive most of the attention in this region, but there are other very interesting cultivars that yield delightful, individualistic red wines that deserve a mention.

Ruché

Ruché is one of these supposedly "minor" varieties, but planted in the proper soils and made in a manner that focuses on its varietal appeal, it makes for an unmistakable wine. It is planted primarily in the Monferrato territory, where seven local towns including Castagnole Monferrato, Grana, Scurzolengo and Viarigi make up the heart of the production zone. There are variations as to how the grape got its name; some say it was derived from the commune of San Rocco, where monks supposedly specialized in this grape centuries ago, while others think it may come from the word *roche*, a word in Piemontese dialect that refers to a vine planted in the Monferrato hills.

Marco Crivelli, who produces one of the most typical versions at his winery in Castagnole Monferrato, notes that while the tannins add weight to the wine, the acidity is very low, around

4.5% (as a comparison, acidity for a Barolo would be about 5.5%), so it is preferable to drink a Ruchè "within its first three years, especially to appreciate its perfumes."

There are various styles produced, some aged only in stainless steel or cement tanks, while others do receive a bit of wood maturation. The Montalbera winery in Castagnole Monferrato specializes in Ruché, producing as many as four versions in a year, ranging from steel-aged to a *passito* offering. The entry level version, named La Tradizione, fermented and aged in steel, displays the spiced cherry, wild strawberry and china bark aromas that make Ruché so distinctive.

This is an easy-drinking wine, and given the richness of a grape such as Nebbiolo, most wine drinkers think Ruché is one-dimensional, meant for immediate consumption. Luca Caramellino, enologist at Montalbera, begs to differ. He speaks of the "mellow and elegant style" of Ruché, but also notes its "sometimes exotic fruit, which can indeed take on spicy tones with time in the bottle."

Caramellino, along with fellow winemaker Andrea Paglietti produce more complex styles, as with their "Laccento" and "Limpronta" versions; the former made from overripe grapes, the latter aged in barrique. These wines display beautiful complexity and rich spice and can be aged for seven to ten years. It is with these wines that the enologists recommend such food pairings as *tajarin* topped with *tartufi* or even a salad with goat cheese. (Other recommended producers of Ruché include Marco Crivelli, Cantine Sant'Agata and Dacapo.)

Grignolino

As for Grignolino, here is a variety that results in a wine with a real seductive quality, if you let yourself in for its allure. Grignolino is a combination of refinement wrapped in delicate marasca cherry flavors, medium-weight tannins and subtle Oriental spices. The pink/pale garnet hue announces its delicate nature, while its tannins give it a slightly bitter edge, making it a fine food wine, especially with lighter *salumi*, simple soups and delicate seafood.

Some examples are quite supple and can be enjoyed chilled, almost as a *rosato*.

Although the total plantings of Grignolino throughout Piemonte are small, there are some renowned producers that work with the variety, arguably the most famous being Braida in Rocchetta Tanaro, known foremost for their outstanding examples of Barbera. Proprietor Raffaella Bologna who has been working with the variety for multiple decades, has recently introduced a new offering known as "Limonte," as the source vineyard is rich in lime (*limo* in Italian). Fermented and matured solely in stainless steel tanks, there are delightful flavors of strawberry with aromatics of rhubarb; medium-bodied with very good acidity, this is one of the classiest and most charming versions that exists today. "Grignolino is a treasure of Piemonte," she remarks. "It's not the first wine people ask for when they visit Piemonte, but it's part of our culture, especially in Monferrato."

Bologna explains that the name of the variety comes from the seeds (*grignole*); she notes that Grignolino contains at least three times as many seeds as Barbera, Dolcetto or Nebbiolo. Because of this, there is a short fermentation with skin contact, to avoid excessive bitterness in the wine; the brief maceration time results in a pale garnet color.

While Grignolino is today an unassuming red that is usually paired with simple foods, it wasn't always that way, according to Bologna. "Once upon a time, Grignolino was a wine of the nobility, where Barbera was for the *paesans*," she comments. "So for the royalty, Grignolino was a wine to pair with soups or refined foods."

The Braida "Limonte" is clasified as a Grignolino d'Asti; other excellent examples of this designation include that of Marco Crivelli, a splendid version that displays an especially floral aromatic profile, as well as those from Montalbera and Spertino. Top-rated examples of Grignolino del Monferrato Casalese (from the province of Alessandria) include those from Beccaria (labeled as "Grignò"), Cantine Valpane and Gaudio Bricco Mondalino; this producer's limited production "Bricco Mondalino" version from vineyards almost 1000 feet (300 meters) elevation is an undiscovered gem.

Also, there are Langhe producers that regularly craft notable versions of Grignolino, including Cavallotto (from their Bricco Boschis vineyard, labeled as "Grign", offering a distinctive note of caraway on the nose), Francesco Rinaldi and Francesco Boschis; these last two better known for Barolo and Dogliani, respectively. Certainly the fact that highly celebrated vintners such as these continue to work with Grignolino is a source of satisfaction for advocates of this variety.

Finally, while most versions of Grignolino are amiable, unassuming wines for short term consumption, there is at least one example that shows how complex and refined this wine can be, when given the proper care. At Azienda Agricola Accornero in the municipality of Vignale Monferrato in the province of Alessandria (Grignolino del Monferrato Casalese), winemaker Ermanno Accornero produces a single vineyard rendering called "Bricco del Bosco Vigne Vecchie" that is simply unforgettable. The fruit is sourced from vineyards planted in 1961, and the wine is matured in French tonneaux for three years, followed by three additional years of bottle age (Accornero also produces a Grignolino "Bricco del Bosco" from younger vines that is aged solely in stainless steel tanks).

Accornero comments that this way of crafting Grignolino is for more or less, "revisiting how this variety was vinified 100 years ago, when the wine was found on the tables of the aristocrats of that era." In Accornero's words, this wine "illustrates all of the characteristics of Grignolino."

Having tasted the 2008 vintage (the third rendition of this wine; only about 1500 bottles are made), at a restaurant in Alto Piemonte in September, 2015, I cannot imagine a more complex, refined and fulfilling example of Grignolino. Offering gorgeous aromas of balsamic, dried cherry and rose essence perfumes, this is medium-bodied with excellent concentration, very good acidity and excellent persistence. 2008 was a superior vintage in Piemonte for red wines, and this wine has the balance and structure for an additional 7–10 years of drinkability. This is a wine of great breeding as well as varietal focus, one with a sense of place as well as *anima* (The 2010, tasted in 2015 is of similar class, but needs another few years in the bottle to display its best qualities).

While it is not as powerful as a Nebbiolo-based wine, I would feel comfortable enjoying this alongside a Barolo, Barbaresco, Gattinara or Boca of the same age-it's of that same superior quality level and served blind, it might even fool a few people who praise those famous reds. If this is indeed how Grignolino was vinified for the aristocracy more than a century ago, those rulers were very fortunate to enjoy this at dinner; thanks to Accornero, a few of us can have the benefit of that same pleasure today. Bravo Ermanno!

Freisa

Freisa, grown in several provinces of Piemonte, is a red that rarely receives much attention, despite its myriad of styles. It can be a dry red, a slightly sparkling *frizzante* or made into a *rosato*. Sometimes it's even blended into Grignolino d'Asti or Grignolino del Monferrato Casalese, where is can be as much as ten percent of the cuvée. Given this data, I guess you can call Freisa a cat-like variety, as it seemingly has nine lives!

The textbook examples of Freisa are bottled under the Freisa di Chieri DOC designation; the production zone includes a small section in the city of Torino, while most of the vineyards are located east of the city. One of the leading producers is the Balbiano estate, managed by winemaker Luca Balbiano. Speaking with him, as he reveals the history of Freisa, is fascinating, as he describes the numerous versions that have been produced over the years in this area. Noting that most examples in the past were lightly sweet, Balbiano comments that "we are now in a period where Freisa is known as a dry wine."

On this topic, Balbiano points out that while Freisa has the reputation of a simple wine—whether produced dry or sweet—it is a difficult grape to work with, due to its natural high acidity, as well as its high levels of tannins. "If you go too long with the fer-

Luca Balbiano, Freisa specialist extraordinaire.

mentation, the extraction of green tannins from the seeds is too high." His method to produce the finest dry Friesa possible is to leave the skins in contact for fifteen to twenty days, extracting all the best parts of the grapes, color, skin and body. Modern technology has allowed Balbiano to make the type of serious Friesa he admires. "Now it's possible, but until the 1970s or '80s, it was quite difficult to vinify a good Freisa."

Balbiano produces six different examples of Freisa, from a *frizzante* version labeled secco, that offers wild strawberry and rhubarb notes, to a *superiore* labeled Il Barbarossa that has very good acidity and charm, to his top of the line Freisa named Vigna Villa della Regina (also a *superiore*). This wine, from an ideally sited vineyard in Torino (the famous Mole Antonelliana building is not far from this plot), is proof that Freisa can be a complex, dry red wine. Offering sour cherry and dried tobacco notes (the wine matures for six months in tonneaux), this is medium-full, with very good acidity, medium-weight tannins, excellent persistence and a lovely suppleness. The 2012, tasted in 2015, should drink well for at least another 5–7 years, perhaps longer.

Balbiano notes that the Villa della Regina vineyard has more calcaire than the clay soils from where the Barbarossa wine is made; "this gives the wine less muscle than the Barbarossa, but maybe more elegance." For the 2012, Balbiano produced a mere 3400 bottles of the Villa della Regina wine; green harvest assures a small crop, while Balbiano's loving care in the cellar ensures a wine of marvelous complexity.

While the soul of Freisa is in Chieri, there are other versions produced under the Langhe Freisa D.O.C.; one of the most representative is from the producer G.D. Vajra, located in the town of Vergne, a *frazione* of the city of Barolo. The family labels this wine, a complex version full of currant and cinnamon notes as "Kyé", which is derived from *Chi é? (*who is it?); this done perhaps as most wine drinkers have no idea of what Freisa is.

Giuseppe Vajra explains that Freisa is actually quite similar to Nebbiolo. He remarks that current DNA studies have demonstrated that, but in his words, "this was the least obvious guess of them all until recently, due to the tedious prejudice against Freisa." He notes how much alike the length of the shoots and the shape of the leaves are for Freisa and Nebbiolo, with the major difference being "the length of the stems."

As for the wine, Vajra points out that the "key feature for Freisa is the malic acidity." Given the high levels of H2M (malic acid) in the variety, the *frizzante* style has become popular among various producers. Vajra explains that his family allows the grapes an extra 15–20 days on the vine, so as to allow a better phenolic rip-

Luca Balbiano produces six different examples of Freisa at his eponymous estate in Andezeno near Torino (if you have the chance, visit this winery to tour the delightful toy museum). Given that the styles range from light, everyday wines to weightier, more ageworthy examples, Balbiano realizes that each version requires different food pairings.

"For the youngest Freisa," he comments," these are easy-drinking, so match them with simple things that you eat everyday, such as salami, cheeses and pastas. For the frizzante version, fried things, so fritto misto, the Piemontese fried dish that is made with meat and vegetables, or the clasic bolito, so boiled meats."

For the superiore versions, Balbiano recommends braised meats or aged cheeses. For the Villa della Regina, he believes that game is the best food pairing because in his words, "it has the spicy sensations, with black pepper and vanilla that matches well with game." He also loves spicy pastas as well as a carbonara with this wine.

ening and decrease overall malic acidity. Regarding tannins, Vajra says that "they are slightly more rustic than those of Nebbiolo."

The "Kyé" is medium-full with moderate tannins and notes of tobacco in the finish; depending on the strength of the vintage, the wine is best consumed from three to seven years of age. As to why a producer of excellent Barolo and Dolcetto works with Freisa, Vajra notes that his father Aldo, who today is the proprietor and winemaker, grew up enjoying Freisa di Chieri at local *osterie* in the Torino area, where he lived in post-war Italy. "It was by chance that he discovered that a well-made, dry Freisa could age longer and with more nuances than a traditional ligher version," notes Giuseppe.

Another Freisa of note is that of Giuseppe Mascarello; their "Toetto" version is from the vineyard of the same name in Castiglione Falletto. Matured in Slavonian oak casks for fifteen months, the wine is bottled two years following the vintage; the Mascarello version often displays slightly more tannins than the Vajra offering, though neither has what you would call a strong tannic edge. Both wines are proof that a serious Freisa from older vineyards can be a wine of great delight and charm and one that can be enjoyed for five years or longer following the vintage.

Pelaverga

The story of Pelaverga is an interesting one, as it is centered around one commune, that of Verduno, situated in the Barolo production zone. However, there are two Pelaverga vines, so the story is twofold.

While the vine planted in Verduno is most famous, there is Pelaverga that originates from the town of Saluzzo in the province of Cuneo, west of Alba. This vine is referred to as Pelaverga Grosso, and it is also known as Cari, in the Colli Torinese hills, north of Torino. Wines made from Pelaverga Grosso are labeled under the Colline Saluzzesi DOC; there is a *rosato* made solely with Pelaveraga as well as a *rosso*, while Pelaverga can also make up a percentage of a Colline Saluzzesi red, blended with other varieties such as Barbera and Nebbiolo.

Regarding Pelaverga from Verduno, it is believed to have originated in that commune as far back as the 1600s, according to Mario Andrion, enologist at Castello di Verduno. "The legend has it that Beato Sebastiano Valfrè, born in Verduno in 1629, brought a Pelaverga vine from Saluzzo to Verduno," he remarks.

Andrion notes that over the course of time, Pelaverga in Verduno was planted alongside Nebbiolo and Barbera; with all these varieties being

Albarossa

A few words about Albarossa, a variety that is a cross between Chatus and Barbera. A handful of producers such as Michele Chiarlo, Banfi Piemonte and Podere Ruggeri Corsini work with it; my only experience with multiple offerings has been with this last producer. Proprietor/winemaker Nicola Argemente notes the polyphenols of this grape, which result in a deep color (deep ruby red/light purple) with rich tannins; there is good natural acidity as well. Tasting through the 2012, 2010 and 2008 versions of this wine (designated as a Langhe Rosso), the wine displays ripe plum and iodine notes when young; after almost seven years, the 2008 offered a nice finesse along with good complexity. Though this variety is still somewhat rare in Piemonte, the wines are improving and if a bit rough, they are ideal paired with roast meats.

vinified together. "Then in 1968, Gabriella Burlotto, from Castello di Verduno, vinfied Pelaverga separately."

Today, Pelaverga from Verduno is referred to as Pelaverga di Verduno or Pelaverga Piccolo; this latter reference, as this plant has smaller berries than the Pelaverga from Saluzzo. Naturally, given its location in the Barolo production zone, Pelaverga from Verduno is much better known as the producers of Verduno have taken great pride in this variety, crafting delightful versions. There are currently about a dozen producers with about 23 hectares planted in the commune (there is also a tiny amount—about one hectare in total-planted in the neighboring communes of La Mora and Roddi).

A typical Verduno Pelaverga displays a garnet color with perfumes of rhubarb, sour cherry and strawberry; there is good acidity, tannins are moderate and there is often a light note of pepper in the finish. This is a wine for the short term and is best paired with salumi or pasta as a first course, while pork or braised rabbit would be an excellent pairing with a *secondi piatti*. The best examples are from Castello di Verduno (who also vinfies a delightful white version known as "Bellis Perennis"–this a *vino da tavola*); Burlotto, Fratelli Alessandria and Bel Colle.

TEN

Sparkling Wine

Italians love sparkling wine, so it's no surprise that this is a vital category in Piemonte. The region's best known bubblies are Asti Spumante as well as the *frizzante* style of Moscato d'Asti, but there are also several beautiful *metodo classico* wines made from grapes as varied as Cortese, Pinot Nero, Chardonnay and even Nebbiolo.

Starting with the *metodo classico* wines, the Alta Langa examples are arguably the region's finest. One of the secrets of these wines is the location of the production zone, one that overlaps three provinces (Cuneo, Asti and Alessandria) in the far southern reaches of the region near the Ligurian border. Here, temperatures are much cooler than in other sections of these provinces where Nebbiolo and Barbera ripen; thus Alta Langa is ideal for early ripening varieties such as Pinot Nero and Chardonnay, which are of course, the base of many great sparkling wines the world over.

The vineyards sit between 250–600 meters (820–1960 feet) above sea level, while the soils are limestone, embedded with many small stones. Danilo Drocco, who makes four different versions of Alta Langa at Fontanafredda, notes that many of the houses here are made of stone and not clay, as in other parts of the Langhe. "In the past," Drocco remarks, the area was very poor, so the only opportunity to build was with what you found in the area." Drocco also points out that as this area is cooler as compared to locales a few miles north, "residents of the Langhe would build their summer homes in Alta Langa to get away from the heat."

Sergio Germano, winemaker at Ettore Germano in Serralunga d'Alba, comments that in the Alta Langa, "we get the Liguria sea air as well as fresh air from the mountains. The limestone soils are ideal for late maturation, for good freshness and high acidity."

Alta Langa must be produced from at least 90% Pinot Nero and/or Chardonnay; in reality, almost every example is comprised entirely of one or both of these varieties. While most versions (there are about a dozen producers) are blends of the two varieties, there are versions that are entirely one or the other; the Giulio Cocchi *Bianc d'Bianc* is exclusively Chardonnay, while the Banfi "Cuvée Aurora" Rosé and the Fontanafredda "Vigna Gatinera" Brut are two excellent examples of Pinot Nero *in purezza*. Minumim aging in the cellar is 30 months, with a Riserva being at least 36 months. Most producers exceed the miniumum, with at least two—Gancia and Enrico Serafino—making a special cuvée that is aged on the lees for 60 months.

The Searafino wine in this case is the Alta Langa Brut Zero, named as it has zero dosage, creating an extremely dry wine. But while other sparkling wines made in this fashion can be slightly bitter or even a bit astringent, the Serafino "Zero" is remarkably elegant with a long, satisfying finish with very good acidity that cleans the mouth and leaves you wanting a second glass. The lengthy period on the lees creates tremendous complexity, resulting in not just one of the best examples of Alta Langa, but one of the finest sparkling wines in all of Italy.

Germano also produces a sparkling wine that is not Alta Langa, as it is made solely from Nebbiolo, which is not allowed in the Alta Langa production zone. "When I started making sparkling wine, I was fascinated by Nebbiolo, as many people say Nebbiolo and Pinot Noir are relatives. Of course, Nebbiolo is a little stronger with more tannins, but if we harvest at the right moment, we have very good acidity and freshness along with excellent varietal character." While sparkling Nebbiolo may seem a bit of an oddity, Germano's version, a Brut Rosé named "Rosanna" is first-rate with aromas of red cherry, strawberry and a hint of white pepper; the perlage is quite fine and there is a nice finesse to the wine. It is also quite delicious and can drink well for 3–5 years after the vintage date.

Lately more producers in the region are producing *metodo classico* sparkling wines solely or primarily from Nebbiolo. At Cuvage in Acqui Terme in the province of Alessandria, enologist Loris Gava produces a Rosé Brut that is 100% Nebbiolo sourced from vineyards in the Barolo production zone. While that may seem a bit odd at first, Gava believes the origins of these grapes are ideal for his cuvée. "The Nebbiolo grape has good acidity as well as a tannic structure that allows for longevity—think of Barolo. A sparkling wine made from Nebbiolo can display beautiful aromas for six to eight years and will continue to evolve in the glass. His Rosé Brut that I tasted at the winery in September 2015 (disgorged March 2015 after 24 months on the lees) displays intriguing perfumes of peony, orange roses and dark cherry, with impressive depth of fruit, good acidity and notable persistence. Best of all, the wine offers a nice sense of finesse.

At Cascina Chicco, near Canale in the Roero district, brothers Marco and Enrico Faccenda produce two *metodo classico* that are Nebbiolo *in purezza*: a Brut and a Brut Rosé. Enrico Faccenda remarks that his brother Marco and he chose Nebbiolo, as it is the grape of their district. "By using this product," he says, we can speak about our terroir using Nebbiolo."

The grapes originate from the Roero district and interestingly enough, they are both Brut Zero, so no dosage. While I like the allure of the rosé, for my tastes the Brut is a better wine, with greater persistence and more varietal character. Aged on the lees for 36 months, this offers enticing plum fruit with a light yeastiness in the aromas, along with excelllent freshness. Very dry, this is one of the most impressive sparkling wines made from Nebbiolo I have tasted to date; most importantly, like the Cuvage wine, this is a sparkling Nebbiolo with finesse. It has been a pleasure witinessing the improvement over the past decade of sparkling Nebbiolo in this region, as these notable examples aim for refinement, not power.

Cuvage also produces a sparkling wine entirely from Cortese grapes, one of the major indigenous white varieties of the region; the wine carries the interesting moniker "Montecarlo Offshore." Gava selected Cortese, as he is "trying to introduce a new concept here of producing a *metodo classico* wine made with Cortese grapes. After all, the world is full of Chardonnay grapes," he states.

Medium-bodied with pleasing papaya, pear and magnolia aromas, this does not have the complexity or richness of his Nebbiolo cuvée, but it does have very good freshness and harmony and is a nice start to this particular project.

Back in the Roero district, Antonio Deltetto and his son Carlo craft several *metodo classico*, including a noteworthy vintage-dated Brut Zero that spends 60 months on the lees. Their finest cuvée however is their Brut Rosé, a blend of Pinot Nero and Nebbiolo; this has the power of the latter along with the fragrance and suppleness of the former. Aged for 48 months on the lees, this offers beautiful strawberry, red cherry and carnation aromas along with a distinct toastiness, which truly sets this wine apart from most of its competitors; this will drink well for three to five years after release. Neither an Alta Langa nor a sparkling wine comprised solely of Nebbiolo, this is a unique offering that shows what can be done as far as crafting Piemontese sparkling wine of enhanced quality.

Other Piemontese *metodo classico spumanti* I have thoroughly enjoyed include the Ariano & Ariano Brut, from Santo Stefano Belbo, a wine with bright fruit and delicate citrus aromas, and the Borgo Maragliano "Giuseppe Gagliano" Brut Riserva Millesimato. This wine, from vineyards near Loazzolo, is a blend of 80% Pinot Nero and 20% Chardonnay that is aged on its lees for three years. The wine offers beautiful dried pear and biscuit aromas and excellent complexity; it is a fine match for river fish and game birds.

Asti / Moscato d'Asti

The most famous and most readily available sparkling wines of Piemonte come from Asti in two different versions: Asti Spumante, which is a *spumante* and Moscato d'Asti, which is slighlty sparkling or *frizzante*. The fact that both are made entirely from the Moscato grape, which is as consumer-friendly a variety as there is, has certainly helped these two wines gain enormous worlwide popularity.

Asti Spumante (or simply Asti) and Moscato d'Asti differ slightly in terms of production, as Asti tends to be slighlty drier with a bit more alcohol (7% or a bit more, as compared to 5.5% for Moscato d'Asti). During the fermentation of Moscato d'Asti, the carbon dioxide that is a by-process (along with transforming the natural grape sugars into alcohol) is absorbed into the wine, making this a *frizzante*, so there is a slight "pop" when you pull the cork.

I mentioned sweetness for these wines; it's important to note that sweetness is a relative term. While Asti is thought of as off-dry or lightly sweet, some versions can be a touch cloying, reminding one more of soda pop than wine. As the aromas and flavors of Moscato, with its zesty notes of orange flowers, tangerine, yellow peach and jasmine are so appealing, many consumers don't mind a bit of sweetness in the wine, as for their palates, this sweetness only complements the fresh fruit of the Moscato variety. This has resulted in too many firms making simple wines that are priced to sell on supermarket shelves. All fine and good in terms of sales and product recognition, but these examples don't offer the promise of how good a well-made Asti can be.

There are some examples however that stand out, as there are a handful of artisinal producers that excel with Asti. One of the best every year is the firm of Romano Dogliotti, located in the town of Castiglione Tinella, in the heart of the production zone. His Asti, featuring a whimsical label by famed artist and grappa producer Romano Levi, is made from his estate grapes that were planted in 1975. Medium-full with very good acidity, this Asti,

Glass and bottle of Ca'd'Gal Moscato d'Asti. Among the finest of its type, this can age for up to a decade in the best vintages.

The Wines and Foods of Piemonte

named "La Selvatica," is simply delicious and so elegant! This is a first-class Asti, very enjoyable upon release or for 12–18 months with many desserts, especially ones that are not too sweet, such as a hazelnut torte.

While much of the Asti that is available these days emerges from large producers, most examples of Moscato d'Asti come from smaller or mid-size wineries. There are numerous Barolo producers, for example that make a Moscato d'Asti, a telling statement as to the regard this wine has in the Langhe. Some of the loveliest versions of these products are from Oddero; Gianni Voerzio; Vajra; Vietti and Batasiolo. Interestingly, while the product is named for the Asti province, a small strip of the production zone is situated in Serralunga d'Alba; indeed the great Barolo firm of Massolino, located here, produces a charming Moscato d'Asti.

Fontanafredda, another renowned estate in Serralunga, has been producing notable examples of both Asti (their "Galarej" is drier and better balanced than many Asti) and Moscato d'Asti for some time under the guidance of enologist Danilo Drocco. His best rendering of Moscato d'Asti is the "Moncucco" bottling, with the grapes sourced from a vineyard in Santo Stefano Belbo, a commune that is all about the Moscato grape. This is a great example of typicity with its appealing—no, let's make that *sexy*-aromas of ginger, peach, apricot and white flowers backed by just a trace of sweetness. While I've enjoyed it with fresh strawberries, I like it almost as much on its own.

Dogliotti, who I mentioned above for his Asti, also specializes in Moscato d'Asti, producing two excellent versions, "La Caudrina" and "La Galeisa." Also look for the brilliant Forteto della Luja "Piasa San Maurizio", which has a bit more weight on the palate than most examples of Moscato d'Asti and can actually drink well for two to three years. Additionally, the limited production "Black Edition" Moscato d'Asti from Enrico Serafino in Canale (Asti province) has striking floral aromas with notes of geranium and orange roses with hints of ginger, lemon zest and sage. If you can find this wine, purchase it right away, as it is a true gem!

Finally, the Ca' d'Gal estate, located in Santo Stefano Belbo, is a great producer of Moscato d'Asti. Managed by Alessandro Boito, there are two examples of Moscato d'Asti crafted: Lumine and the Vigna Vecchia. This latter wine is an amazing example, a rare ageworthy Moscato d'Asti. I tasted the 2011 release in September 2015 and was taken by its varietal purity with lovely floral (magnolia) and fruit (white peach and yellow apple) perfumes, as well as its freshness; four years old, the wine seemed as though it was brand new. Offering impeccable balance as well as great charisma and finesse, this is an outstanding Moscato d'Asti and a must try for anyone who wants to experience the heights of this wine type.

Brachetto d'Acqui

Brachetto d'Acqui is a charming, slightly sparkling, slightly sweet wine made from the red Brachetto variety. It has several things in common with Moscato d'Asti, most notably its low alcohol (5.5%-6%) and the fact that it is made in the *frizzante* style, with a light touch of sweetness.

The production zone is situated in two provinces, Alessandria and Asti; there are eight communes, such as Acqui Terme and Alice Bel Colle, in the former, with eighteen communes, including Loazzolo and Nizza Monferrato in the latter. Numerous firms in these towns produce a Brachetto d'Acqui as well as a Moscato d'Asti.

This is a delightful dessert wine that is simply delicious, ideal for a hot summer's day by itself, or paired with strawberries, simple *biscotti* or lighter chocolate *dolci*. The typical version, known as Birbet in the Roero district, is meant for enjoyment early on, even as young as six months after the harvest. Recommended producers include Braida, Cantina Alice Bel Colle, Bera and Tenuta Il Falchetto.

ELEVEN

White wines

While the red wines of Piemonte are the most radiant examples of this region's viticultural brilliance, there are several notable white wines from this land that are first-rate.

Arneis

Arneis, meaning "rascal" in local dialect, is a wine that has become a recent phenomenon. It was in the late 1960s that Alfredo Currado at Vietti produced what is thought of as the first example of Arneis. His son Luca recalls that these grapes were known at the time as 'nebbia bianca' and that they were planted in among the rows of Nebbiolo. Currado decide to vinify these grapes separately and after doing so, left the wine to rest in his cellar; when he tasted the wine several months later, he was pleasantly surprised at its richness and complexity.

It took a few years, but soon a few other firms made their own examples of Arneis, two of the most famous being Bruno Giacosa and Ceretto, both famed producers of Barolo and Barbaresco, just like Vietti. Today thanks to the notoriety of these producers as well as its attractive qualities as a medium-bodied, dry white with elegant aromatics, Arneis has become a major success.

Arneis is characterized by its perfumes of pear, melon and golden apples along with floral notes of peony, chamomile and

Massimiliana Spinola, biodynamic Gavi producer,
Castello di Tassarolo.

acacia. Sometimes a touch of honey will emerge in the nose, as is
the case with the "Imprimis" version from Ghiomo, while wines
that have been in the bottle for two to three years will offer a note
of almond in the aromatics. Most versions are unoaked to emphasize the grape's fragrances; acidity is very good, though like most
whites from Piemonte, not exceedingly high.

While there are some excellent versions of Arneis from the
Langhe district where red wines such as Barolo and Barbaresco
are most famous, the best-known versions of Arneis today are
from the Roero district in the province of Cuneo. The Roero is

The Wines and Foods of Piemonte

located just across the Tanaro River from the Langhe and while Nebbiolo is used for an excellent local red known as Roero Rosso, this wine never gets the attention of its more famous Nebbiolo-based counterparts from the region.

Thus it is Arneis that has brought the most attention to Roero, especially over the past ten to fifteen years, as plantings have increased on a large scale. The best examples of Roero Arneis, such as the classic bottling of Matteo Coreggia, "Trinita" and "Saglietto" from Malvirà, Malabaila "Pradvaj" or the Marco Porello "Camestri" (these last four cru offerings), express excellent depth of fruit and texture, often with a note of minerality in the finish; stellar examples such as these have an aging potential of five to seven years or even longer in the best vintages. The uncomplicated stylings of Roero Arneis, combined with its freshness make this an ideal aperitif; it is also marvelous when paired with lighter seafood, poultry, pork or risotto.

While few consumers think about it, Arneis can age and develop greater complexity with a few years in the bottle. I tasted the 2010 "Cecu d'la Bionda" Roero Arneis from Monchiero Carbone with proprietor/winemakers Francesco Monchiero in late 2015; this offered notes of banana as well as a pleasant nuttiness. I also noted a hint of petrol, which Monchiero also found; "After five years," he remarked, "this Arneis evolves in a special way. For me, it's similar to a Riesling." Pointing out that consumers in Europe and America greatly prefer one or two-year old Arneis (and nothing older), Carbone mentioned that in Japan in late 2015, the wine drinkers there were enjoying the 2011 and 2012. "It's a challenge for us, to make people understand that Arneis can age. But if you have an *insalata russa* with a five year old Arneis, it's perfect."

Gavi

It was once true (and may still be) that easy- to-pronounce names were responsible for an Italian wine's success; that certainly was the case for Gavi throughout the 1980s and 1990s. While this wine's market share has decreased over the past two decades—no doubt due to the recent interest in Arneis as well as the success of Pinot Grigio from numerous Italian regions-the quality of Gavi has rarely been higher, thanks to the diligence of a few dozen artisan producers.

Gavi is produced in the province of Alessandria in southeastern Piemonte and is named for the eponymous town; in total there are eleven communes that encompass the Gavi production zone; Bosio, the southernmost of these is situated at the border with the Liguria region. Produced entirely from the Cortese grape-the name means "courteous" in Italian—Gavi (sometimes labeled as Cortese di Gavi) is made as a dry table wine as well as a sparkling wine (both *frizzante* and spumante); there are even a few estates that produce a dessert wine made in the *passito* method, although this is not technically defined as a Gavi.

Certainly the typical steel-aged version can be a courteous, rather friendly wine with its pear, quince and spearmint aromas; a note of almond often emerges with time.

Magda Pedrini of the eponymous firm in Gavi notes the distinctiveness of this wine, remarking that, "when correctly made, Gavi has a freshness, sapidity and minerality that certainly could be appreciated by those who drink fine, dry wines of high quality." Marco Castellari Bergaglio of Castellari Bergaglio who produces seven different versions of Gavi (five of them dry, still wines), notes the natural acidity of the Cortese grape and understands the aging potential of Gavi, especially when produced from older vineyards and reduced yields. "All of our production has a long life," he comments. "Many people think you must drink Gavi young, but it's not true. You can drink it young, but you can also age it.. some examples drink well after five or six years."

Many producers make two or more examples of non-oaked Gavi; usually the more serious version is a *selezione* of the oldest vineyards. A notable example of this is the "Bruno Broglia" offering from the Broglia estate in Lomellina, a hamlet just north of Gavi; produced from vines planted in the early to mid-1950s, this offers impressive richness on the palate along with a lengthy fin-

The Wines and Foods of Piemonte

Sergio Germano, Ettore Germano. His "Herzu" Riesling is one of Piemonte's finest white wines.

ish; this is a Gavi that has the aging potential of a decade or longer from the best vintages.

While steel-aged Gavi is a delight, it is only one face of this white, as several smaller estates ferment and/or mature their versions in small oak barrels; notable producers include Castellari Bergaglio ("Pilin"), Fontanassa ("Vigna du Citù") and Villa Sparina ("Monterotondo"). Marco Bergaglio of Castellari Bergaglio admits that the use of barriques for Gavi is difficult, "as Gavi is so delicate, so the oak can be dominant." Because of this, he waits one additional year to release his "Pilin" bottling for sale; this has been a wise decision, as the final result is a wine with added texture from barrel aging, with very subtle wood notes that remain in the background.

There is also a movement in Gavi to appply biodynamic practices in the vineyards and cellar; leading estates adopting this philosophy include La Raia and Castello di Tassarolo. At the latter estate, co-proprietor Massimiliana Spinola converted her 20 hectares to biodynamic viticulture because, in her words, "I strongly believe this to be the only solution to heal our earth and to give the consumer a product that brings health and vitality."

Since taking over the production at her estate following her father's death, the yields are 50% less; Spinola emphasizes that the vines are in balance and the wines display "more purity and harmony." There are several examples of Gavi produced here, all of them quite subtle, offering beautiful harmony, most notably in the "Alborina" bottling, sourced from a single estate vineyard, and the "Titouan"–named for one of the heavy horses that Spinola and her husband employ to work the soil—that is aged in older barriques and has no added sulfur dioxide.

Riesling

Riesling in Piemonte? Well there isn't a lot of it, but there are at least two excellent versions in the Langhe, both somewhat surprisingly from Barolo producers, namely Ettore Germano of Serralunga d'Alba and G.D. Vajra in Vergne, just outside the town of Barolo.

Starting with the former, Sergio Germano decided to work with Riesling for one simple reason—it's his favorite white grape. His challenge was to locate the right conditions for the variety in the Langhe; he found it in the small commune of Ciglié, a few miles south of Dogliani and the commune of Barolo. Starting in 1995, he planted the grape on a visually stunning plateau some 500–550 meters (1640–1800 feet) above sea level on white chalky limestone soils laden with stones. He used a selection of German clones from the Rheingau and the Mittelrhein; this as a result of his love for the Rieslings from these areas.

His Riesling, which he labels "Herzu" is quite rich with striking aromatics of stone fruits—apricots and peaches—along with notes of petrol, lime and geranium. Steel-aged and in contact with its lees for six months, this is a Riesling that displays lovely freshness, very good acidity and a subtle touch of minerality. The emphasis is on elegance, not power, so this is a wine for medium-term drinking, say five to seven years, although ten years is not out of the question.

The Vajra version, named "Pètracine" (stone roots) is sourced from two vineyards, one in the commune of Barolo with gravelly-sandy soils and the other from the small town of Sinio, situated near Serralunga d'Alba; the clones are a mix of German and Alsatian plant material.

This is a delicate version of Riesling, one with marvelous perfumes of petrol, melon, green apples and chamomile. This is a bit more delicate than the Germano version, offering lovely finesse and balance; consume this within three to five years of the vintage date, though the best vintages can be enjoyed for a few more years.

Erbaluce di Caluso

From northern Piemonte, in the Canavese area a bit northeast of Torino, the small town of Caluso is the center of the production zone for wines made from the Erbaluce grape. Naturally high in acidity, Erbaluce is made in several versions, ranging from sparkling to dry table white to *passito*. Whatever the style, Erbaluce rarely fails to disappoint; hopefully it will be discovered outside of its territory as one of Italy's most prized indigenous varieties.

Taking a look at the vineyards in the zone is something special, as it seems you have been transported back some five or six decades. Many of the vineyards are in small blocks—this is not an area of spectacular hillside plantings with vines as far as the eye can see. The predominant system here is pergola, where the canopy is overhead, so as to protect the berries from excessive sun and ensure a longer growing season (the name of the local system is *pergola canavesana*).

The name erbaluce is derived from two Italian words, *erba* (herb), referring to the wine's herbal notes, and *luce* (light), for its brilliant color as a young wine. Most producers make stainless steel-aged versions as well as an example aged in wood. The former is the more typical style, with the newly released wines displaying perfumes of spearmint, lemon rind, chamomile and yellow flowers. Some *selezioni* from older vineyards, such as the Orsolani "Vignot S. Antonio" (barrique-aged) or the "Misobolo" from Cieck (stainless steel only) tend to offer aromas of sage, rosemary and almond in addition to the the typical fruit notes. These latter wines are among Piemonte's most intriguing whites, as they have marvelous complexity, mineral notes and can drink well for five to seven years after the vintage; they are especially wonderful paired with local risotto with asparagus.

Regarding Erbaluce *passito,* I have written about these sweet wines in the chapter on *dolci,* which appears later in this book.

Timorasso

Timorasso is an indigenous variety planted in the Colli Tortonesi district, named for the town of Tortona in the province of Alessandria. While it has enjoyed a good deal of fame over recent years, it has actually been planted for centuries; Anna Manfredi of Vigne Marina Coppi reports that the first agrarian encyclopedia written by Pietro de Crescenzi in the 14th century listed Timorasso as the main variety of the Tortonesi area.

The variety was disappearing, however, toward the second half of the 21st century, due in great part to the cost of labor in working with this grape in the vineyards (the variety is a low-yielding one). It was Walter Massa in the village of Monleale who has been credited with rescuing Timorasso from extinction, as he planted the variety in the early and mid-1990s.

Today, Massa is somewhat of a reference point for Timoras-

Francesco Bellochio and Anna Manfredi, Vigne Marina
Coppi, producers of Timorasso and Favorita.

so, producing four versions, three of which are cru offerings; all of
these are labeled under the Derthona DOC designation (Derthona
is the old name for the city of Tortona), while other local producers
use the Colli Tortonesi DOC terminology. His wines are remarkable; a prime reason being that he gives the grapes skin contact
for 60 hours. The thick skins of Timorasso make this possible and
give the wines added richness as well as tannins that contribute to
the aging potential of this variety. His cru offerings include "Mon-

tecitorio" and "Sterpi"; the former being more delicate, while the latter displays greater intensity.

Another celebrated producer of Timorasso is Vigne Marina Coppi, situated in the town of Castellania. Their version of Timorasso is known as "Fausto," named for the world-class cyclist of the 1940s and '50s, Fausto Coppi, grandfather of current proprietor/winemaker Francesco Bellocchio. The grapes for this wine are sourced from vineyards 400 meters (1300 feet) above sea level; soils are calcerous of Sant'Agata marne, which lends a distinct minerality to the wines. Harvest takes place at the beginning of October.

The 2010, tasted at a restaurant in Barbaresco in late 2014, showed brilliantly with aromas of acacia, papaya and guava; the wine is matured solely in steel tanks to emphasize its varietal purity (the wine also received lees stirring for eight months). Medium-full with superb texture, the wine displays great minerality, so much so that its style resembles a Premier Cru or Grand Cru Chablis. This was one of the finest whites of Piemonte that I had ever tasted; it certainly was one of the most complex and explosive.

During a visit to the Marina Coppi estate in September, 2015, I tasted the 2012 with Bellocchio and his wife; this is another outstanding wine that has the depth and ripeness of the 2010, but will need more time in the bottle before it displays the minerality and breadth of previous vintages.

"Timorasso became the 'big white' of Piemonte," says Bellocchio. "Sometimes I say it is close to Barolo, as you can age it. The technical aspects are that it has good tannins, higher alcohol (the 2012 has 14.5% alcohol) and high acidity, so it is perfect to age."

Bellocchio, a driven individual, is learning incrementally about Timorasso; what it is and what sort of potential it can display. "Every year gives you more evolution," he remarks. "Timorasso is on the market two years after the harvest, but you should drink it when it is eight to ten years old." While he would prefer to release his Timorasso a good five or seven years after the vintage, he realizes he has to compromise a bit. "It's important to have wine in the market, even if we have to make a sacrifice, since we're not Chateau Margaux!"

Both Bellocchio and Manfredi recommend *baccala* with Timorasso, while she also enjoys pairing it with shellfish and *tartufi bianchi*, these last two ideal complements to the richness and class of this enthralling white.

Favorita

Favorita is not seen much outside Piemonte, yet there are excellent versions, if you know where to look. The grape itself is the same variety as Vermentino, most famously cultivated in Sardinia and Liguria, as well as the Maremma district of coastal Tuscany.

Thus Favorita performs best in a cooler climate; in Piemonte, the best versions originate not from the Langhe, where most examples are rather plain, but instead from the Roero as well as the Colli Tortonesi zone. Due to a quirk in the local *disciplinare* regulations, even the versions of Favorita that originate from Roero vineyards must be labeled as Langhe Favorita, as the Roero denomination can only be used for Arneis for white wines (and Roero Rosso for red wines, which is 100% Nebbiolo). Thus one must know the producers and their origins before selecting a Favorita.

A fine starting point would be Deltetto, an underrated estate in Canale, run by Antonio Deltetto and his son Carlo. The younger Deltetto notes that the Favorita harvest is just after that of Arneis, and that the alcohol for Favorita is usually moderate, in the 12.5%-13% range, with the occasional 13.5% in the hot vintages. "That's not something we want," says the younger Deltetto, "because you lose the acidity and freshness." Offering lovely perfumes of mango and orange blossom, the Deltetto Favorita is a delight!

Another lovely example is that from Marco Porello, another Roero producer. His Favorita is imbued with beautiful perfumes as well as very good weight on the palate; there is very good acidity and a delicate saltiness on the finish. Lees stirring adds texture;

while this would be best enjoyed within two years of the vintage date, the finest versions could age for another year or two.

A third notable Favorita from the Roero is the "Onorata" from Angelo Negro. This downplays the tropical fruit stylings of the Porello, in favor of aromas of pear, green tea and even a subtle hint of rosemary. Offering excellent persistence and a distinct salinity in the finish, this is a first-rate Favorita, one that again, should be consumed young, at two to three years from the vintage date. But the complexity of this wine will surprise anyone that believes Favorita is a simple summer sipper.

The most exceptional Favorita I have tasted is the "Marine" from Vigne Marina Coppi in the Colli Tortonesi hills, not far from Liguria. While there are lovely fruit aromas, there are also some strong herbal overtones, such as rosemary, basil and pine that constitute the expressive perfumes. "We are in a wild area," says winemaker Francesco Bellocchio. "We have trees, we have many herbs, I don't think it's a romantic image. I think that the plants around the vineyard give something to the wine. I think there is a little touch of balsamic in the aromas."

As for the fruit, I noticed a strong sense of petrol, as in a Mosel Riesling. Bellocchio agrees, noting that when he was fermenting the 2012 Favorita, "one of the cellar workers was on top of the tank and said to me 'this is Riesling.'" Bellocchio notes the difference in soils in the Colli Tortonesi area as compared to the Roero. "With our soils, this type of marl, Favorita has these characteristics—more body and being capable of being aged for a longer period of time."

Bellocchio notes that he likes to harvest his Favorita grapes in oreder to have a wine, "not drinkable in a year, but if you want, five or six years." Six months of batonnage and lengthy aging in the bottle (the 2012 vintage was the current release in 2015) aid in giving this wine its potential for longevity. Medium-full on the palate with outstanding persistence, this is a great wine and truly one of the undiscovered jewels of Italian white wine!

Bellocchio and his wife love to pair the wine with baccala

and anchovies, two salty dishes that marry beautifully with the flavors of this marvelous wine.

"It's very difficult to communicate what Favorita is," he says. But when people taste it, they change their minds." A typical humble statement from a grower that has made an extraordinary version of something most people think of as ordinary.

Nascetta

Nascetta, or Anas-Cëtta, is one of Piemonte's most distinctive whites, made from the eponymous grape grown primarily in the commune of Novello. Generally aged in steel to highlight the pear and tropical fruit perfumes, it has excellent acidity and the structure to age well; Valter Fissore of the Elvio Cogno estate, who produced the first commercial example in 1994, says that "without a doubt, it can age for ten years . . . at that time, the minerality starts to emerge."

Fissore admits that the exact origin of the variety is a mystery, although some suggest it came from Sardinia; he does think it has much in common with a Mediterranean white, as he describes the "notes of rosemary and sage."

Only a few dozen wineries work with Nascetta; others from Novello include Le Strette, Stra and Vietto; Braida, a famed Barbera producer, has recently begun work with the variety from their estate in Costigliole d'Asti.

TWELVE

Dolci

Piemonte may not be famous for its dessert wines, but there are at least two excellent examples that are quite memorable: Moscato Passito and Erbaluce di Caluso Passito.

Beginning with Moscato Passito, most examples are made from slightly to very overripe Moscato grapes harvested at the end of September or early October, although picking can finish as late as mid-November. One of the best versions, that of Forteto della Luja, is made from overripe grapes that have been affected by the botrytis rot, causing the grapes to shrivel on the vines. These grapes are then placed on straw mats to continue to dry—only 15% of the grapes are treated in this manner for the Forteto della Luja version—after which fermentation takes place in small oak barrels for approximately two years.

The finished product has a golden orange/amber appearance, with perfumes ranging from the typical local Moscato fragrances of orange blossom and apricot to honey and almond. Medium-full, the best versions have the proper acidity to balance the lushness of the ripe, fat fruit. Ideal pairings include simple biscotti as well as such heavenly sweets such as caramel gelato or *zabaione* (zabaglione). Recommended versions include those from Forteto della Luja and Borgo Maragliano (these two labeled as Loazzolo DOC, meaning they are produced from grapes grown

in the eponymous city in the Asti province) as well as Olim Bauda (Moscato Passito Piemonte). Given the proper conditions, with
wines from a vintage that offered good acidity, a Moscato Passito
can drink well for 12–15 years.

Erbaluce Passito

Erbaluce is another variety in Piemonte that is made as a *passito*;
many producers that make a dry Erbaluce di Caluso also craft a
sweet version. As mentioned earlier when I discussed sparkling
wine, Erbaluce has very good natural acidity, making it not only a
fine variety for a bubbly, but also a dessert wine as well.

The Erbaluce grapes are harvested and then placed on mats
in the sun or an attic to dry; some producers may hang them from
racks in a temperature controlled room as well; drying time is normally between four to five months. The shriveled, deeply concentrated grapes, now affected by noble rot, are then fermented in
wooden barrels, usually small, but sometimes as large as 25 hectoliters. Aging takes place for three to four years, during which the
casks are topped off, to help prevent oxidation.

The resulting wines, released anywhere from five to ten
years after the vintage, are deep amber in color, with lush apricot, honey and *créme caramel* flavors, and a rich, medium-sweet
finish that is substantial, but not overly sweet, thanks to the excellent acidity of the Erbaluce grape. Best examples include the La
Campore, Orsolani "Sulè," and the Cieck "Alladium" and "Alladium" Riserva; while these are rich enough and delicious enough to
be enjoyed after dinner as a *vino da meditazione* on their own, they
are also wonderful paired with almond pastries or blue cheeses.

There are other examples of *passiti*, made in small qunati-
ties. These include Brachetto *passito*—look for Marenco "Passrí"
and Bragnagnolo "Passione"—and Gavi *passito* (usually labeled as
vino da tavola as there is no Gavi Passito DOP designation); excellent versions include Castellari Bergaglio "Gavium" and Cascina
degli Ulivi.

Barolo Chinato

Unless you have enjoyed dinner in Piemonte, chances are you are not familiar with Barolo Chinato, one of the region's most enchanting wines. This is a Barolo that has been infused with China bark and blended with a recipe—each producer has his own secret mixture—of medicinal herbs and spices. Aged for several years, the resulting product is medium sweet, with an alcohol level around 16%. While some in the area consume it as a digestif, it is most commonly served after dinner, sometimes with an orange peel, but most frequently neat, as a vino da meditazione. I have ended numerous meals in Piemonte with a Barolo Chianto, sipping it slowly, enjoying its distinctive characteristics, as it is a perfect ending to another glorious day in Piemonte. Top examples include those from Cappellano, Rocche Costamagna, Marcarini and Fontanafredda.

Malvasia

Briefly, one last dessert wine from Piemonte: Malvasia di Castelnuovo Don Bosco, an appealing, uncomplicated, lightly sweet wine made from a red variety that is a lot of fun to drink!

The Malvasia wine is named for the city of Castelnuovo in the province of Asti; the variety is Malvasia di Schierano. "We have lots of Malvasias in Italy," says Luca Balbiano, who works with the variety at his eponymous family firm north of Torino, "but this is the only Malvasia vinified as a sweet wine." After a soft pressing and brief fermentation with the skins, Balbiano refrigerates the wine to reach the desired alcohol, which is 5.5%. Displaying a pretty young garnet color and delightful aromas of candied red fruits such as strawberries and red cherries, along with notes of red roses, this is fresh and delicious (note that it has a lively mousse when poured, as this is technically a *frizzante* wine. I am listing it here in the *dolci* section as it is relatively unknown and I wanted to give this wine its due).

Balbiano recommends serving this wine chilled at about 8°C (45°C), so as the perfumes are fully enhanced; pair with strawberry or marmalade cakes, crème-filled pastries or *biscotti*. Other fine examples include those from Marchesi di Barolo, Terredavino "Valsera" and Bava "Rosetta."

The Wines and Foods of Piemonte

PART TWO

Interviews with Producers

Alessandro Ceretto, Ceretto, Alba

Alessandro Ceretto is the winemaker at the famed Ceretto family estate in Alba, having assumed the mantle from his father Marcello and his uncle Bruno. Best known for the cru offerings from sites owned by his family in both the Barolo (Bricco Rocche, Prapò) and Barbaresco (Asili, Bernadot) production zones, he has recently refined the style of the wines, opting for more natural farming as well as less small oak in the cellar.

Alessandro Ceretto

When did you assume winemaking duties at Ceretto?

"My first real harvest was 1996, but I traveled around a bit, so 1999. But consider that in 1999, I was 23 years old. Then I kept studying the harvests, so I consider my real first harvest 2005 or 2006.

You're going back to botti and getting away from barrique. Is that because you believe barrique was a trend or it didn't give you the best results?

"I traveled around the world and botti exists only in Italy, I believe. I was young, so you start to drink wine when you're 20 or 21 before you get wisdom, before you get a big ground of knowledge as far as what you're doing or knowing the peculiarities or characteristics of an area or wine, it takes time.

"The real reason the barrique appeared in the winery is you have to consider the big jump in generations. Between my grandfather and father, it was from demijohns (50 to 52 liters-70 bottles of wine) to bottles. From not having vineyards to buying vineyards. 100 years ago, no one was thinking that you have to own 100% of your sites.

"In my case, my father was working at the winery in Alba that he inherited from his grandfather. When my grandfather built the winery, there was no water. So the cleaning of a winery was not even an option.

"Then in the 1990s, we moved. But there were still some botti remaining at the old winery. So there were some that had not been washed in 60 years, so they were getting mold. This mold was characteristic of everywhere.

"Today, you can still find a wine that when you put it to your nose, the smell can be linked to a particular cask. This is rare and you can count the number of examples on one hand, but it still occurs . . . It's a wet wood smell, sort of a mushroom smell.

"Imagine you have a winery with botti and you get wines with these aromas. You blame it on the botti. There's no question that you can get great wine from botti, but I didn't have any. My father at that time in 1980, 1990 and up to 2000 was like many others and used barrique. I think at that time the belief was that the quality of the wine was due to the winemaker.

"Now it has been understood virtually everywhere that the quality is because of the vineyard and then a good winemaker. But a good winemaker doesn't mean you get good wine. As a winemaker, you walk with it from the vineyard to the bottle. But it isn't massaging the wine or being a strong winemaker.

"In that period, everyone was comparing, but at that time, the law required two years of aging Barolo in oak. Another thing—how many great wines from around the world over the course of time spend two years of aging in barrique? Very, very few. They start from twelve months in Burgundy, maybe a little bit more and they can reach sixteen months, eighteen months and you can find some wines as long as two years, but that's usually with different sized casks.

"I don't like the quality that oxygen gives to a wine for two years-it's probably too much. Barolo was there. It was overoaked and overoxidized. Those are things you can understand after two or three harvests. At the beginnining, you can blame it on one harvest being too hot, for example.

"But with continuous results, you say, no, it's the barrels. Nebbiolo is aggressive when it is young, so you need to massage it bit. But for me the solution is a little time in barrique, because you need the oxygen and then you have to stop because the oxygen 'presses the accelerator' on the nose and goes the same speed on the mouth.

"When you don't have many more aromas to develop, you put the wine on the nose and you get a nose that seems seven years old and a mouth that seems three years old. You have a body of a young guy and your head is fifty years old or the opposite.

"So for me, the balance comes from using barrique as is necessary, but don't try to round the tannins. Don't try to force it, to try and make a Cabernet or Merlot or Syrah that is more round. Don't push the tannins, because if you do, you will have problems with the nose. That doesn't happen with botti.

"This is the reason I am now back with the botti. I had the experience of vinfying in botti to understand that the barrique is too much. To reach my final interpretation, no more new oak or really very, very little . . . You have to use the two containers."

Compared to Burgundy and Bordeaux, are prices of Barolo and Barbaresco too low, given their quality?

"If you think about it, it is the market that makes the prices. Yes, Barolo and Barbaresco are somewhat undervalued, but as we have been making great strides with these wines the past few years, the gap in pricing will close.

The problem is that we don't have an appellation system that certifies wines as grand cru, premier cru, first growth, second growth, etc. That being the case, the French wines will always have the advantage as far as esteem in the marketplace."

Luca Currado, Vietti, Castiglione Falletto

Luca Currado enjoyed an enviable education in winemaking, as he worked with his family in the vineyards and cellars as a young boy. Today, in his mid-40s, Currado has succeeded his father Alfredo and has made Vietti into one of the most formidable and successful wineries in the Langhe, thanks in part to his progressive nature, as he has expanded the winery's portfolio by purchasing sections of some of the finest cru in the Barolo zone over the past decade.

Luca Currado

The Wines and Foods of Piemonte

How are the wines different today than from what your father made?

"Not very different. I think today we are lucky because during the period of my father and other wineries, they were struggling; it was not a period of richness like today.

"Also, they were selling wine, but it was not like today. They did not have temperature control; the first temperature control we installed in the summer of 1980.

My father was always considered a traditional producer, but I don't like using this classification because it is basically incorrect; it depends on which vineyard you have. We are lucky, as we have so many *grand cru* vineyards, so we can tailor the style of vinification and aging according to the characteristic of terroir. We have vineyards in Serralunga, Monforte, in Barolo and Novello.

"What my father was trying to do, what I'm trying to do is not make a Luca style or an Alfredo style. I think it was something where we step back and do the style of the vineyards. So we have always been very traditional but we never saw tradition as a static world. You're always learning, it's an evolution."

Tell me about the Barolo vineyards you work with, such as Lazzarito in Serralunga, Rocche in Castiglione, Brunate in La Morra, etc.

"We are lucky because what I consider the 20 most important *grand cru* in the Barolo zone, we own at least a piece of 15 of them. So this has allowed us to have incredible diversity and to have an incredible operation.

"I always divide the Barolo region into three major hills. I always consider Barolo as a shape, a football with three slices. There is the slice of Serralunga, the slice of Barolo, Castiglione Falletto and Monforte and the slice of La Morra, Verduno and Novello.

"Serralunga always makes a Barolo that is masculine and very powerful, very intense with great minerality with a full nose, with white pepper. It is a wine that reminds me of the Côte de Nuits because of the spice. There is Lazzarito, Vigna Rionda, Cascina Frata. It is always a Barolo with intense tannins. They need to ripen well. So Lazzarito is our Châteauneuf-du-Pape.

"Then we go to the opposite side with La Morra. La Morra always makes a Barolo that is more elegant, more feminine. Thank about Brunate, think about Cerequio, think about Rocche dell'Annunziata—they're all perfumed. The wines are very elegant with tannins that are round and they become velvety so they are drinkable a little sooner than the others.

"Castiglione Falletto is in the middle. It's in the middle also in terms of characteristics. You think about Rocche and Villero—they combine the power of Serralunga with the elegance of La Morra. These are always wines with an extremely long life, but they are always very balanced.

"Castiglione for me, especially the Rocche vineyard, is like a Swiss watch, a masterpiece with twelve complications, so when everything comes together, it is an incredible Barolo.

"Brunate on the other hand is our Sophia Loren of Barolo—a wine with some personality but great perfume, you know, a strong woman. So this for me is the difference."

What are your thoughts on the producers that attempted to make a more "modern" Barolo?

"Twenty years ago, there were many Barolos with a lot of oak, very concentrated. Maybe it was a good wine, but it was something different than Barolo. We were always portrayed as stupid, Bartolo Mascarello, Beppe Rinaldi, ourselves and all the traditional producers. We were always looked upon as stupid people. Then those people that considered themselves modern style, now they're traditionalists!

"This is stupid, this is not correct, this is a big mistake. Because if you trust in what you do, you do not have to change. I think maybe in twenty years, maybe the modern style will again be in fashion, so they will go back again. It depends on how the wind blows.

"And so anyway for us, today as well as 30 years ago, 40 years ago, 50 years ago, it has always been about terroir."

Danilo Drocco, Fontanafredda, Serralunga d'Alba

Danilo Drocco is the wine-maker at Fontanafredda, a position he has held since 1999, after moving from the Prunotto firm in Alba. He combines both traditional and modern techniques in his cellar practices and is considered one of the most talented enologists in the area; his work with wines as varied as Barolo, Moscato d'Asti and Alta Langa are testament to that.

Danilo Drocco

Over the years, how have you changed the way that you make Barolo?

"My background was and is the most important part of my job. I had the opportunity with Beppe Colla (at Prunotto) to work and understand the philosophy of making wine in the most traditional style. Then in the second part of my work at Prunotto with Antinori, I could try the new style of making Barolo. So traditional style using only big casks, racking only if it is necessary, but not racking too much. The second way, using barrique. So making the wine, managing more the oxygen. I started without (using barrique) and I finished with using barrique."

For your Barolos today, you start the aging process in barriques and then finish matuaration in botti, correct?

"Yes, when I arrived I had to make a difficult decision because Fontanafredda was known around the world as an ancient traditional winery. There was the movement of the Barolo Boys. It was very easy to follow the commercial direction of the Barolo

Boys, so wine with a lot of new oak, wine with a lot of fruit. The problem is that it was not the right 'dress' for Fontanafredda. So I tried to find a middle road. Because people had an idea of Fontanafredda as a traditional winery.

"So I decided to use my knowledge of using the oak and for having cleaner wine, with richer fruit, but not too oaky. The first approach for me at Fontanafredda was to age all the Barolo in barrique for the first year and then in big casks for the second year. Then to go immediately in the bottle as soon as possible.

"I decided to follow this technique because the proper way of using the barrique is to keep and increase the color of Nebbiolo. And if you use the barrique properly, you can also increase the taste of fruit. Thanks to my experience at Prunotto, I could understand how much better it was to use barriques of second or third passage, so immediately I started to buy barriques that I used for Barbera and the second year, I started to use them for Barolo. I used perhaps 25–35% new, but primarily used barrique. It depends also on the vintage; the richer and more powerful the wine, the higher percentage of new barriques you can use."

Are the Barolos of today better than in the past?

"Yes, generally the wine is better because thanks to journalists that permitted us to know that in the world and in our area there are people that can make wine better than me! I remember 20–30 years ago, every producer used to taste only his own wine; there was not the habit of doing comparison with others. Now we taste and compare Barolos as well as other wines of the world. This is an exercise that permitted us to understand where it was possible to improve.

"The knowledge—everybody talks about the increase of the quality of the wine, but the increase in the quality of the wine depends in my opinion of at least 90% of the increase in the quality of the grape. We did a great job with the grapes. The grapes I crushed 15 years ago are completely different now in terms of talking about quantity of grape per vine, maturation of

The Wines and Foods of Piemonte

the tannins. Now it's much much better, as now we have more knowledge of these qualities."

You produce Barolo from the communes of Serralunga as well as Barolo. What are the differences?

"There is a logical difference. You know the history of this area, there was the sea. When Africa crashed against Europe, the Alps went out and this part of the territory and this level of the sea went up. The area of Serralunga was the first to come out from the sea. So geologically, it is the most ancient soil of the area. We talk about millions of years of difference between the area of Serralunga and the area of Barolo. You can imagine in millions of years of difference of age, the rain washed the soil. The final result is a poorer soil with a great quantity of calcaire (lime-stone), so it is a soil that can give wine with a stronger quantity of tannins and grapes that grow with greater difficulty.

"In Barolo, the soil is younger. So it is richer. We are talking about little differences, obviously. In Barolo, in the Paigallo vineyard, like all the other cru of the area, the soil is a little richer. There is also a little more humidity. So thanks to the water, the vines can develop a little more easily. Barolo offers a fruitier wine with beautiful aromas, very elegant. Serralunga is a wine very rich with big body, big structure of tannins and more complex aromas. I love to say that in Serralunga, we have wines that taste of the earth. After two to three years of aging, we have wines that have aromas of tobacco, drying leaves, mushrooms-that is very typical of this area."

Gianluca Grasso, Elio Grasso, Monforte d'Alba

Gianluca Grasso is the wine-maker at the visually strik-ing Elio Grasso estate in the commune of Monforte d'Al-ba, where he works with his father Elio and mother Marti-na, carrying on their work of traditional cru Barolo with the Ginestra Casa Maté and Gava-rini Chiniera releases. Gianlu-ca also crafts a barrique-aged

Gianluca Grasso

Barolo blended from these vineyards; produced in the best years, this is a *riserva* Barolo called Rüncot.

Tell me a little bit of your family's history.

"I'm the 3rd generation. My grandfather was Romano Grasso. He was born in 1887. At the beginning, he used to sell grapes to the main producers in the area; he would also sell the wine in barrels.

"My father Elio in the 1970s, decided to stop selling grapes and wine in kegs and bottle 100% of the wine made from grapes on our property. In 1996, when I finished my studies, I joined my family here at the winery. All of the family is involved in this business. But this word business-this is not a business, this is a passion! It is a job you can do only if you have passion. Without passion, it's better you do something else."

What does Barolo mean to you? How special a wine has it been in your family?

"Don't forget this, Dolcetto in the past was a wine that was at our table everyday and still is. The wine Barolo in some ways was like meat. Not every single day did they have beef on the table, maybe once or twice a month, maybe on Sundays.

"Barolo is a special wine and in my opinion, you can drink Barolo every day, but if you drink it on a special occasion or you drink it with the people you really love, it's much better. Barolo is a wine that puts me—Barolo is a wine that puts people together to talk, to have fun. And then when you drink a bottle of Barolo, when you put your nose in the glass, when you taste the wine, if you close your eyes, you must have a journey in our area. You must experience our terroir."

Tell me about your work as a winemaker.

"Wherever I go, people ask me, are you the winemaker? I tell them yes, I am the winemaker, but the most important thing here in this area is the fact that you don't need the winemaker, but you must be a great grape grower—that's the key. That's point #1–only with great grapes are we able to make great wines. If the grapes are just okay, then the wines will be just okay. The goal of the winemaker, the goal of the people that work with the grapes is to maintain and be able to transfer the DNA of each single vineyard, each single terroir to the bottle. When you drink a bottle of Barolo from Monforte for example and you can taste the minerality, the earthiness from Monforte, then our goal has been achieved."

Tell me about your decision to make a modern style Barolo that is different from the traditional wines of your father.

"Rüncot is my 'son.' The Gavarini Chiniera and Casa Maté are wines my grandfather and father made and today I am still making these wines in absolutely the same way. In 1996 when I finished my studies, I told my father that I wanted to make something based on my studies. Rüncot is between Gavarini Chiniera and Casa Maté; the wine took 50% of the minerality of the Gavarini Chiniera and 50% of the clay of the Casa Maté. If you take the clay and look in your hands, they are completely different pieces of soil. Casa Maté soil is much more brown, while Chiniera soil is much more white. We have a lot of chalk here. Rüncot is "located" in the middle, so it is a 50% Chiniera, 50% Casa Maté wine.

"This wine is aged in French barrels for 45 to 50 months, sometimes even a little longer. The aging is done in our caves, completely underground at 14 degrees Celsius and 90% humidity. The wineries in the past were built with a natural humidity—that is the best way, in my opinion, for aging.

"This wine is a *riserva*—we release it after seven years. By law, to call a Barolo a *riserva*, it can be released after six years, but for the 2007 and 2008, we released this wine one year later."

Finally, tell me about the passing down of heritage, of tradition, in Barolo and in your family.

"My generation is different than my father's. I always trust in the people before myself. My grandfather, my father and now me. I am doing the same things they did. Of course, I don't have the same barrels they had, but I am making the wines the same way."

Franco Massolino, Massolino, Serralunga d'Alba

The best word I can use to describe the wines at this outstanding Serralunga estate is precision; every wine is singular, a glorious representation of its origins. Franco Massolino, a thoughtful, soft-spoken individual is the co-winemaker here, while his brother Roberto manages the vineyards. The approach here is a traditional one, with aging in large casks; these are Barolos that display admirable restraint as well as exquisite harmony.

Franco Massolino

The Wines and Foods of Piemonte

Tell us about your winery.

"Our business was established by my great-grandfather more than 100 years ago. Step by step, my grandfather and uncle and my father Giovanni together specialized in production of Serralunga wine. We sold our wine in tank, in big barrel, but step by step, we started to bottle the wine and sell it with our name. The first bottle we produced with our name was in 1947.

"You know that around the turn of the 20th century, phylloxera destroyed 90% of the plants in this area. It was a difficult sitation in this area for economic situation during the two World Wars, so it was very difficult for the families to work and honestly, even eat. They produced vegetables and also wine.

"But the situation is totally different from today. Today we are working in a high level of quality. We are working all together to show the highest possible quality in this area."

How have your Barolos evolved in style over the years?
How have they become more elegant?

"I think Barolo is a wine that has become more elegant. We would like to produce a wine that has the great balance between power—that is the DNA of Nebbiolo- and elegance; this is something that only the greatest varieties in the world can show. It's always a question of balance. There are vintages that need to age and there are vintages that are able to show their balance and complexity even when they are young.

"I remember when I was young, the Barolos of the 1960s and '70s were nearly undrinkable when they were young. It was not important if they were produced in a modern way or the traditional style. They were wines that were very hard, because often the tannins were not ripe.

"So today a majority of the producers invest a lot of work in the vineyards, following every small detail to lead to perfect conditions. So we get ripe fruit along with big tannins, but the wines are already elegant.

"This is the big change in my opinion in this area over the

last 25 or 30 years. Generally speaking, traditional producers like us are able to make wines that are no longer closed, tannic, acidic—wines that are nearly undrinkable for 20 or 30 years.

"In my opinion we have to work in this direction to explain to people that if you are able to choose the right vintage, you can have the great pleasure of enjoying a Barolo that is only five or six years old and you don't have to wait twenty years before you enjoy a glass of Barolo."

What do you consider the signature, the thumbprint for Serralunga Barolo?

"In Serralunga, we have geologically the oldest soil. It is the only area in Barolo where you can find iron oxidation in the ground.

"Generally in Serralunga, we have great deepness, we have unique complexity. It's not only a question of tannins, because we are also working with a vineyard from Castiglione Falletto (Parussi). The tannins from Castiglione Falletto are so much like our Barolos. In quantity they are probably the same.

"I think Serralunga has something special in the soil. It yields wines of complexity, deepness and elegance."

Does Barolo get the respect it deserves?

"If we are able to work together well, Barolo has a wonderful future. It's a wine that is unique in the world. "If you are looking for only a good glass of wine, you have a lot of choices. In every country you can enjoy a good glass of wine. But if you would like to enjoy a unique glass of wine that has a distinctive expression, so if you are in a blind tasting, in my opinion, it's absolutely easy to recognize Nebbiolo because it has its own its character. There is no similarity with any other variety.

"From the viewpoint of wine producers, it's incredible. You can produce a wine that you would like and you can have a unique expression. So the style of Massolino is different than the style of Elio Grasso, which is different than the style of Bruno Giacosa which is different from the style of all the other producers.

Because we are working with a sensitive variety in which we can change the style of the bouquet with small changes in vinification or in the soil. Each producer can have his own expression, his own unique style."

Mariacristina Oddero, Poderi Oddero, La Morra

Poderi Oddero, located in the La Morra *frazione* of Santa Maria, is one of Barolo's most history-laden and well-respected producers. The first bottle of Oddero Barolo dates back to 1878; today Mariacristina, who holds a degree in agronomic sciences from Turin and a Masters in viticulture and enology, is a co-proprietor and winemaker at this estate. Besides being one of the area's most knowledgeable vintners, she is a delightful person; my interview with her offered valuable insight into the Oddero operation along with great insight into how this dedicated producer achieves their goals.

Mariacristina Oddero

You produce a classic Barolo as well as several cru offerings. When did you begin making cru bottlings of Barolo?

"We started to produce Barolo cru in 1982 with Rocche di Castiglione and Vigna Rionda. Before, my father Giacomo and his brother produced only Barolo *classico* made from different vineyards from La Morra, from Castiglione, from Serralunga. We started bottlings the single vineyards in 1982, one from Castiglione Falletto, one from Serralunga, after the suggestion of Luigi Veronelli.

"After, they continued with other vineyards such as Bussia in Monforte d'Alba and then my team group and I continued with Villero and Brunate."

Can you compare Brunate and Villero?

"We started to produce Brunate in 2004. We have a very small vineyard in the highest part of Brunate, less than one-half an hectare. We decided to have the single vineyard selection because it is a fantastic vineyard. In the past, we used these grapes for the classic Barolo. My father bought a section of Brunate in 1968. His brother and he used the grapes in the Barolo *classico* because they thought it was too small to have a single vineyard.

"It is the highest part of the Brunate vineyard near the town of La Morra. The microclimate is fantastic because there is always a fresh breeze and it is not too windy. There is less problem with insects (moths) than in other areas and the vineyard is well ventilated, so the humidity is low."

Is Brunate the best vineyard you have?

"It's very famous, it's true. But we are lucky, as we can produce Bussia Vigna Mondoca and Villero and others, so it is difficult to say that Brunate is the best or Rocche di Castiglione is the best. All of the vineyards are our children. I like Brunate, but I also like Rocche."

Do you think that by producing cru Barolo that it helps you in the marketplace?

"My father thinks that Barolo *classico* is the best solution because in his opinion, it is made with the best grapes of La Morra, with the best grapes of Serralunga, with the best grapes of Castiglione Falletto, so it is perfection. It's not a stupid idea, as it could be the very best expression of the vintage.

"My father still believes to this day that this is the best expression of Barolo. But I think we are lucky because we can produce Barolo from different areas, with different terroirs, with different microclimates. We are quite fortunate to have grapes from different areas. Because we are such a strong heritage, because we own such strong vineyards with important characteristics, with different characteristics . . .

"It's sort of a waste not to give a voice to this specific character. The beauty of wine is to see the same grape give such varying personalities simply because of different soils and different microclimates. So we wanted to give voice to these vineyards and we decided to use the most historical vineyards.

"We still continue to produce classic Barolo because we believe in this tradition of this region. We don't want to forget, we don't want to abandon this approach."

Are you happy with the ways that Barolo is being marketed today?

"Not always. For example, in Italy, often not. I see great interest from foreigners. Sometimes foreign people when they come here, they are very knowledgable about Barolo and they want to learn more. They ask me very intelligent questions.

"I was in Milan recently and the owners of resturants asked me stupid questions!

I think as far as discussing Barolo with other producers, today it is a little easier than in the past. I see when we have tastings around the world, it is a nice comparison."

Pietro Ratti, Renato Ratti, Annunziata, La Morra

At his stunning winery that clings to a hillside in the Annunziata subzone of La Morra, Pietro Ratti continues the work of his father Renato, producing some of this area's most distinctive Barolos. Equally important in defining this man however, is his tireless work as a promoter of all of the wines of the Langhe and Roero districts. He was instrumental in the successful effort to have the Barolo and Barbaresco zones recognized as World Heritage Sites by UNESCO, which was announced in June, 2014. He

Pietro Ratti

also believes very strongly that Barolo is not given its proper due among the world's greatest wines.

Describe the terroir of Annunziata.

"Annunziata is one of the most extraordinary subzones of La Morra. It is as big as Castiglione Falletto; there are about 30 wineries here. The Annunziata zone is a special terroir, so if you think of the wines from La Morra as elegant, the wines from Annunziata are really elegant.

"It's the soil plus the elevation, here we are looking at about 1000 feet elevation, so it's not too high, so all of the wines made here are very elegant."

Tell me about the particular characteristics of your
Barolos from Annunziata.

"Conca is always the most powerful Barolo that we make here. It's full-bodied and the tannins are strong but fine. Conca is a small vineyard, less than ten acres, just below the winery. Conca means "shell"; you always feel the heat of the place. This is always a full-bodied, front mouth and robust style of Barolo.

"Rocche dell'Annunziata is interesting to taste alongside Conca, as they are made in the same way. The vineyards are not too far away. Rocche is on the other side of the hill with a little more southwestern exposure. The soils have a little more sand, clay and limestone, while Conca is blue clay soil, so the soils of Rocche dell'Annunziata are a little more complex compared to Conca.

"Rocche is very elegant, very refined. It is very different from Conca. Conca has more balsamic notes and sweet flowers. Rocche is the most Burgundian wine we have in the Barolo area. It's extremely elegant, the old vines give this wine extra length— the finish goes on and on.

"For Marcenasco (a blend of Annunziata vineyards), we get a package of aromas and structure. Marcenasco is about balance, Conca is about power and Rocche, complexity and elegance."

What do the producers of Barolo need to do to make the
general wine trade more conscious of these wines?

"Barolo is a strong name. But we have to go beyond that. We have to establish names like Conca, Rocche and La Rosa (a Barolo from the Fontanafredda cru in Serralunga d'Alba). These wines are higher in price, but they are made in smaller amounts. They are made in exclusive amounts and more and more people want exclusivity."

Regarding price, are Barolos priced too low?

"The top Burgundies are way more expensive than our Barolos. My hope is that Barolo will be even more expensive in the future, even more than now. Of course, that is the hope for any winery. Barolo in general is undervalued.

"What we need to do is work on the prestige, to make people more aware of Barolo."

Paola Rinaldi, Az. Agr. Francesco Rinaldi, Barolo

Established in 1870, the Francesco Rinaldi winery is situated at the Cannubi hill in the commune of Barolo. Continuity and consistency have been keys to this firm's success, as the wines are made in the same traditional style as was practiced throughout the 20th century. A visit to the cellars may lead you to believe you have traveled back in time as it appears that except for a few pieces of new equipment, you are witnessing how wine was made several decades ago. Paola Rinaldi, one of the most pleasant and charming people

Paola Rinaldi

I've met in Piemonte (the sun always seems to be shining when I see her), has been working for her family estate for more than twenty years, dividing her time between the cellars in Barolo and the offices in the nearby town of Alba.

You produce cru Barolo from two of the most renowned vineyards, Cannubi and Brunate. Please tell me about these wines and their differences.

"For both of these vineyards, the exposition to the sun is the same, as both of them have a southeast exposure.

"One difference, of course, is the ground. Brunate is a little

The Wines and Foods of Piemonte

higher, but it is not a big difference. Our vineyards are nearly 300 meters above sea level. Cannubi is a little lower, but that is not the main difference." (Author's note: Cannubi is situated in the commune of Barolo, while Brunate is located in parts of both the Barolo and La Morra communes.)

"The primary difference is in the soil. Usually when we taste the wines, we taste Brunate before and then we taste Cannubi. This is because Cannubi has slightly harder tannins than our Brunate and needs a little more time to age."

Has climate change affected these two vineyards?

"For 2014, we are returning to the past! There is no climate change this year, as it was very cold in July and August. Each vintage is different—when you ask my uncle who is almost ninety, he will tell you the same thing about every vintage being different.

"This year for Cannubi and Brunate, as they have excellent positioning to the sun, the work will be a little easier compared to other vineyards that do not receive as much sun.

"We produce our wines the same way in the cellar as we did fifty years ago. Of course, we have a little more modern technology now, so it's easier to work, but the style of the work is the same."

Some twenty years ago when the Barolo Boys were changing production methods and receiving big scores in important wine magazines, were you ever tempted to change your style?

"15 or 20 years ago, new customers were looking for international Barolo. So we had to say, "we don't have an international Barolo, we have Barolo." Now I think the modern Barolo producers are not as modern as 20 years ago!

"We have always produced wine in the same way. I have my Barolo. Our customers were asking for the old style of Barolo. We did make changes, as we purchased new barrels, so we eliminated the old wood. But the new barrels are all Slavonian oak. So we do have something new in our cellar, but not the way we produce the wines."

Tell me about your job specifically.

"Yes, our cellar is a small, family-owned cellar, so we have to do many things. Sometimes I work in the cellar, sometimes I work in Alba where we bottle the wines. Sometimes I work in the office in Alba. My sister works in the office. My grandfather bought this house in Alba close to the train station because 50, 60 years ago, the wines were sold by train. That's why our offices are there."

What did your uncle Luciano teach you about Barolo and this land?

"You know, in the beginning, it was not easy. 50 years ago, a woman working in a wine cellar, was not like today. I started in economics in Torino and finished in 1992, so before I helped in the cellar and when I finished studying, I started working. But at the beginning, it was a little difficult to think that here in Barolo a woman was working in the cellar, so it was not easy. But it was possible."

Enrico Scavino, Az. Agr. Paolo Scavino, Castiglione Falletto

One of the Langhe's most celebrated estates is that of Paolo Scavino, situated in Castiglione Falletto. This is a true family affair, as proprietor Enrico Scavino is ably assited in production and sales by his daughters Elisa and Enrica. The family has holdings in some of the most celebrated *cru* in Barolo, including Rocche dell'Annunziata in La Morra, Bricco Ambrogio in Roddi and Monvigliero in Verduno; another great cru that is the source for arguably their

Enrico Scavino

most famous Barolo is Bric dël Fiasc in Castiglione Falletto. In total, they own 23 hectares (56.8 acres) of vineyards from a total of 19 Barolo cru.

Are Barolo and Barbaresco undervalued as compared to Burgundy and Bordeaux?

"The prices for our wines are not as expensive as Burgundy or Bordeaux, yet the quality is extremely high. More people are becoming more passionate about Barolo. For us, it's a fortunate thing in a way, that those wines are priced so expensively, as more people are watching our area.

"The farmers here are keeping their land and in some cases, starting new wineries in order to keep these grapes. In five or ten years, if we maintain them correctly, they will have the same value as Bordeaux or Burgundy. But fortunately for us, we can still offer value for our wines.

"The great quality of Barolo is easily recognized; even children in this area recognize Barolo. This makes us really proud . . . There are many important wines everywhere in the world. But many of these wines do not have the 'important' sensation of the wines of our area.

"Fortunately, we do not blend a wine to fit what the market is requesting. It's a unique area, Barolo. Burgundy has great wines as well, but in many cases, the prices they are asking are far greater than what the market can bear.

"It's nice because at the moment, we are fortunate. France has lovely wines, great wines. The are starting to commercialize their wines in a good way. They have gotten together to promote their wines and let people know what Burgundy is. Now the people from Barolo are starting to get together and promote the area. Before we were working one by one—sort of a 'my wine is better than the one you're producing' way of thinking."

*Please tell me about your work in the vineyards and
winery with your family.*

"Some wineries have agronomists, winemakers and others; they
are set up as an investment, but here, there's only myself along
with my two daughters. There is no agronomist. I am working
the vineyards, so our touch comes from the heart.

"I still have to figure out what I have to do. I need another
sixty harvests. I am 75 years old and I have done this work since I
was 10 years old with my father. You never stop learning.

"Each year is different; it's almost like a new experiment
you have to carry each year. When this becomes just a business,
it will be a very sad situation."

Can you describe the differences between some of your cru Barolo?

"The Bricco Ambrogio is our lady Barolo. The Monvigliero,
meanwhile, is our Iron Lady Barolo, while the Bric dël Fiasc, a
vineyard that is 80% sand and 20% limestone is a Barolo that
has both masculine and feminine traits."

What can you tell me about climate change here in Barolo?

"Now it is easy to find many great Barolos. Twenty years ago it
was so difficult; the wines were having a few problems. So this
change in climate has actually been a good thing for the area."

Roberto Voerzio, La Morra

Roberto Voerzio first produced wines under his own label in 1982, having learned the trade from his father and grandfather in La Morra. His brother Gianni and he set out on their own with each producing cru Barolo; Gianni preceding Roberto in this aspect. While Gianni produced one single vineyard Barolo (from La Serra in La Morra), Roberto produced several from this commune, releasing as many as seven different cru offerings per vintage throughout the 1990s and 2000s. His

Roberto Voerzio

fame was cemented when some of his Barolos received 100 points from a number of influential wine publications.

While there are some that describe Voerzio as a modernist in terms of Barolo, this is largely an incorrect notion. While a few of his wines are aged solely in barrique, he has been using *botti grandi* for many years. There are many strengths to his wines, Barolo as well as Barbera, Dolcetto and Langhe Nebbiolo; arguably the feature that makes his wines so distinctive are the remarkably small yields he achieves in his vineyards.

What is the difference between the wines you make today as opposed to twenty or thirty years ago?

"I can only speak for myself, as each company has its own methods, but for me the work in the cellar is largely the same as when I started twenty-five, thirty years ago.

"I wasn't influenced by the new methods. Each year I

produced different wines, some aged in botti and barrique, some aged only in barrique.

"The big change was in viticulture. Twenty years ago, we were bringing in fruit at 1.5 kilos per plant. Now we are as low as 500 grams (.5 kilos) per plant for our Barolos.

You know, very few noticed our initial changes in our viticulture. This was due to climate. The weather changes ever year, so the wines were and continue to be different every year.

"The changes always take place in the vineyard, while the work in the cellar is the same. Fermentation is always between 20–25 days. I'm doing things the same way my grandfather was doing."

There has been so much written about how you only use barriques for your various Barolo, but this is not correct.

"We purchased barriques every year, but it wasn't until 2004 that I made a Barolo with only new barrique. This was due to the fact that we had no wine in 2002 and not much in 2003, so when 2004 arrived, we had a lot of barriques that had not been used.

But over the years, we have consolidated our wood program and we use barrique—today about 30% new—as well as *botti*. By using these 15 and 20-hectoliter casks, we have achieved a better balance in our wines."

Today, I produce only two Barolos that are aged solely in barrique: Sarmassa and Torriglione. The Capalot (e Brunate Riserva) Barolo was also aged exclusively in barrique, but the 2011 was the last year for that wine."

Do you think that Barolo is undervalued as compared to the great wines from Burgundy and Bordeaux?

"The problem here is in many ways, in the mind. On this question, I am forced to say, 'Viva La Francia'! In France there are thirty or so *domaines*, some with Chardonnay, others working with Pinot Noir that maintain the same level of excellence for all their wines. This is true whether it is for a high or average quality production.

The Wines and Foods of Piemonte

"Here in Barolo, this is true for ourselves and only a handful of other producers, names such as Giacomo Conterno, Aldo Conterno and Bruno Giacosa. As opposed to this, here there are some producers that make a 30 Euro Barolo and now they are also making a 7 Euro Barolo.

"That's why I say 'Viva La Francia'. This doesn't happen in France. Over 100 and 150 years, their wines, named for a vineyard, have become world-renowned. But here we have only Barolo, which is a 'generic wine.'"

Barolo is a generic wine?

"There can be a 7 or 8 Euro Barolo. For a wine such as this, the pricing is correct, because of the quality of the particular vineyard. All of the work with fruit from such a vineyard is not worth the higher price. These wines should probably be labeled as Langhe Nebbiolo, because for me, these wines are not Barolo. These wines are standard production and their quality is mediocre. People will not pay 15 or 20 Euro for a cheap wine.

"We should not be selling Barolo, but instead we should be selling Cerequio, La Serra, Brunate, Cannubi, etc. But everything is Barolo and there are too many mediocre Barolos."

Can you tell me your thoughts on the tradition of Barolo?

"The tradition of Barolo is very simple and practical. For us, tradition is tied into the territory. The historical vineyards planted to Nebbiolo, vineyards such as La Serra, Brunate, Cannubi, Ginestra in Monforte, Monprivato in Castiglione Falletto, these are the ones that best signify Barolo.

"These wines are Barolo, not Langhe Nebbiolo. These are wines that need long fermentations, not three days. The tradition over fifty and one hundred years in the *cantine* is evidence of this. Yields must be low each year to permit the finest wine.

"We now work with high density vineyards to give us the highest quality fruit. Previously when we had lower density, we made good, consistent wine. The consumer must pay a premium for Barolo in a restaurant, so they will not pay premium prices for average quality.

"It's very simple. Each year is different, but we must constantly improve on quality. Now with climate change, it is a challenge, as some wines that were 12% and 13% alcohol are now 14% and 14.5%. Conditions are always changing, but we must continually make great wine.

"Great wine comes from the great vineyards. We do what we can in the cellar to maintain this quality. But the tradition of Barolo does not change—ever."

Giovanna Rizzolio, Cascina delle Rose, Barbaresco

Giovanna Rizzolio, along with her husband Italo Sobrino and their sons Davide and Giovanni, manage Cascina delle Rose, a splendid Barbaresco estate situated in the Rio Sordo *sottozona*. The wines produced at this firm, from Dolcetto and Langhe Nebbiolo to their cru Barbaresco-Rio Sordo and Tre Stelle—are exceptional, offering outstanding varietal purity as well as a dedicated sense of place.

Rizzolio is a captivating individual who is both a wonderful host at her bed and breakfast at the estate, as well

Giovanna Rizzolio and her husband, Italo Sobrino

as a very opinionated woman who has specific ideas about many subjects, be it winemaking or local bureaucracy.

What was your first year of production?

"We first made wines in 1998 and 1999 at another cellar we were renting. We started producing Dolcetto in 2002."

Did you grow up at this estate (Cascina delle Rose)?

"Yes, this was our summer house. My grandmother and my grandfather used this during the summer. Every summer we would stay here for three or four months with my brother and sister, as were living in Alba.

"My father was a farmer and had hazelnuts, but also a stable with about thirty cows. This was really the classic farm with all the things you need as a family.

"I married Italo in 2022, but we were living together since 1997. From 1992 to 1997, I was alone, managing the vineyards as well as the bed and breakfast. But I was younger and I was able to do this!

What is Italo's background?

"Italo's first job was at another winery years ago. Then he changed completely, working in other firms while he was also helping his family with grapes, as they had some vineyards. He knew about wine, thanks to his job at this other company, about forty years ago."

As far as Barbaresco itself, do you think it is not appreciated enough, especially compared to Barolo?

"I think that Nebbiolo is an incredible grape and it is growing so well in the Barbaresco area and Barolo area as well as other areas in Piemonte. They are two completely different types of wine. It's really not possible to compare them, because of the soils. It's not so much the exposition, but rather the soils.

"We have completely different types of wine. It's impossible to compare them. Barolo is more famous, for sure. But we don't have a problem in this way, as Barbaresco, step by step, is becoming known around the world.

"Many people love Barbaresco because it's often easier to drink than Barolo. It's possible to drink Barbaresco at a normal dinner. For Barolo, normally, you need food that is a little more important. Barbaresco is very easy to drink, especially with an elegant dish such as risotto and this is again because of the soil. It's not because we're more elegant than Barolo."

What are Italo and you most proud of here at Cascina delle Rose?

"Italo loves to work; he needs to work. He's not able to stay quiet or sit down. He's working in the vineyards and in the cellar a lot.

"In the beginning, he was arriving here in the evening after his job at the other winery. Then we started to make the wine together. The rest of the day, he was working in the vineyards and cellar also.

"At the end of the day, it's great to have this combination, as he's a big enthusiast. He loves his job and all the things around, especially with the bed and breakfast as well. He's very open and friendly and it's no problem for him to do anything. He's really very open in this way."

Is there one thing you enjoy the most with your work?

"The biggest love for me is working in the vineyard. You have the oxygen for your brain. Vinification is very nice, it's interesting. In the cellar, it's very interesting. You can see the wine growing up, but in the vineyard, you have nature."

Aldo Vacca, Produttori del Barbaresco, Barbaresco

Aldo Vacca serves as Managing Director for the Produttori del Barbaresco, the great cooperative producer in the town of Barbaresco. He was born in Barbaresco in 1958 and has been with Produttori since 1991.

Can you tell me a bit about your wine experience before coming to Produttori del Babraresco?

"I moved with my family at age two to Alba, where my father was working in the export department of the Ferrero chocolate company. I spent my summers and most weekends back then helping my uncles in the vineyards.

"I graduated from the University of Torino in 1982 in the

Viticulture and Oenology Department with a thesis on Neb-biolo clone selection. Soon after, I did some part time work at Produttori and then spent six months at UC Davis in California (one of America's leading wine programs, *author*); upon return-ing to Italy, I worked at Gaja from 1986–1990 and then moved to Produttori, first as export manager and then later as overall Managing Director."

You have commented that in certain vintages, Barbaresco can be a bigger wine than Barolo. Can you explain that?

"Barbaresco can be just as tannic and complex as Barolo, but it is usually lighter on the middle palate. This lighter body some-time gives to Barbaresco an even stronger tannic feel than Barolo which is often rounder. So if big refers to body, yes Barolo can be said to be bigger than Barbaresco. If big refers to tannin and complexity the statement is not correct. The reason is of course the terroir which varies in both areas and therefore can give lighter or bigger wines in both areas in the same way."

What are your instructions for your growers? Do you have many? Or do you let them make their decisions (as to when to harvest, overall yield)?

"We have now 50 growers and they are totally independent in their decision. However, we often meet, at least 4 times a year, and we are always available for consulting if they need help. We always have one big meeting in June when we look at how the season is shaping up, if there are some sanitary issues, how green harvest should be done and so on. When it comes to harvest time, we decide together in another big meeting, the day that we will start, but they can decide when to pick different lots according to their best knowledge. They are paid upon quality at delivery so they make sure to deliver different plots at the best time in order to get better results and higher dollar per pound."

Has climate change affected the commune of Barbaresco and the work of your growers?

"Climate change is making our summers start later and last longer to the effect that both September and October have been, in the last 20 years, drier and warmer than in the previous 50 years. Result is higher alcoholic level in the wine, riper tannins and fruit, overall a better average quality for wines and vintages and somehow an easier life for farmers themselves. Reaching enough ripeness and avoiding bunch rot, the two big issues for Nebbiolo here, are now much easier to handle and achieve."

In general, do you think that the price of Barbaresco and Barolo is too low compared to the great reds from Burgundy and Bordeaux? Or are your wines priced fairly?

"I think that the best Barolo and Barbaresco can stand side by side with the best of Burgundy, quality wise. Price however is a function of so many more variables than just quality and it is usually more difficult for Barolo and Barbaresco to hit big in new markets where wealthy people are willing to spend huge money and were Bordeaux and Burgundy always arrive first. All considered I do think that Barolo and Barbaresco are fairly priced in general and that Produttori del Barbaresco is extremely fairly priced."

Giuseppino Anfossi, Ghiomo, Guarene

Giuseppino Anfossi is the proprietor of a small, artisanal estate named Ghiomo, situated
just across the Tanaro River,
a few miles west of Alba. He
is best known for his Arneis
(labeled as Lagnhe Arneis and
not Roero Arneis, due to the
vagaries of the local *disciplinare*), but also crafts excellent
versions of Barbera, Nebbiolo
and Brachetto. Down to earth
with a cheerful attitude, Anfossi's wines are as direct and
honest as he is.

Giuseppino Anfossi

*Tell me about your estate and
family history.*

"My family has been producing wine for at least five generations.
I have been trying to change our philosophy by elevating the
quality of our wines. Since 1999, I have been bottling the entire
quantity of our production, which is divided among three and
one-half hectares of Nebbiolo, three hectares of Barbera and two
hectares of Arneis. *"Siamo contadini da sempre e orgoliosi di esser-
lo!"* ("We've been farmers forever and we're proud of it!")

*You produce excellent examples of Arneis. What can you tell me
about this variety as well as the versions you make?*

"Arneis was initially planted in the nineteenth century in vineyards that bordered sites containing Barbera and Nebbiolo. It was
there to preserve the red grapes from the attacks of the bees, as
Arneis ripened earlier than these two varieties.

"I think it became famous because it is one of the few
whites wines from our land, a wine that is fresh and easy-

drinking in an area of long-lived reds. With the passage of time, we have improved a lot with Arneis; while working on our red wines, maybe we have learned to make a great white wine, as we have focused on the acidity."

Tell me about your various Arneis.

"Arneis Fussot is more classic fruity and fresh, as it is macerated on the skins for a few hours.

"Arneis Inprimis is more floral with higher acidity with a light sapidity. The grapes are from a very old vineyard; we make a long maceration on the skins and a battonage that can last several months. It is a wine that can age very well for a few years-I think you've tasted the 2008 and is still a nice wine !!

"I hope that my wines have character and are an expression of the vineyards of Guarene, which is very similar to La Morra, a land full of gray marl suitable for wines that can age. Among my favorite vintages are 2008, 2010, 2011 and 2013."

What are your favorite food pairings with Arneis?

"*Pesce di mare e di fiume* (fish of the sea and the river), white meats such as chicken and rabbit, grilled vegetables as well as creamy, but not too strong cheeses such as that from Bra."

You also produce a wine called Birbet, made from Brachetto grapes. What can you tell me about this particular wine?

"Brachetto is an aromatic variety present in the Roero. There is a sub-variety of Brachetto with long bunches that is partially fermented. This is called Birbet and not Brachetto, as that term is used only in the zone of Acqui. The word *birbet* in Piemontese dialect means a person that is very lively.

"Our Birbet is lightly sweet with low alcohol (5.5%) and is an easy-drinking wine for all consumers. It is especially perfect with sweets and fruits, especially great with peaches and strawberries."

Raffaella Bologna, Braida, Rocchetta Tanaro

Together with her brother Giuseppe, Raffaella Bologna manages the famed Braida property in a small village in the province of Asti. They are continuing the work of their father Giacomo, who was one of the revolutionary producers of Barbera d'Asti, when he decided to change the landscape of this wine forever in the early 1980s, aging the wine in small barrels, aiming for a Barbera that instead of being a simple red for immediate consumption, would be a wine with great aging potential. The first Barbera of this

Raffaella Bologna

type was the Bricco dell'Uccellone, from the eponymous vineyard, which was immediately hailed as a great wine and is still regarded in that fashion to this day.

Raffaella is an engaging woman, very energetic and always positive, someone who has continued the amazing success of her family winery while never forgetting her humble origins.

Can you share some of your memories of your father when you saw him working in the vineyards? Also, what are the best memories of him?

"I decided to be involved in wine since I was really young, I think when I was five or six. The things that impressed me most, was that at the time, Braida was producing a wine that we still make, but in a different way, called La Monella. It's a sparkling, *frizzante* Barbera. At the time, it was refermenting in the bottle. We were sleeping at home and in the cantina and it was boom, boom, boom, the bottles were exploding.

"What really shocked me as a kid was to see my father opening a bottle and placing the bottle next to his ear, listening to the wine. I thought my father was drunk! My father told me that you have to listen to the liveliness of the Barbera in the bottle. I thought this was magic!

"When I went to the winemaking school in Alba, the mission again was refermentation, to select the yeasts with my name and to referment the Barbera without big explosions and capture the greatest result in terms of aromas.

"This is a memory that for me combines a memory of my father and the profession I choose to follow.

"A memory of my father that is not necessarily related to wine? He told me to love where you are, but to be part of the world. When I was very young my brother and I, he sent us outside to make comparisons and give us an education of curiosity and critique, so that we were able to find our own way. Unfortunately we had to find our own way, because I was 18 when he died. He passed away in December, 1990; he was 56. My brother Giuseppe and I were just coming out from the wine school in Alba and had then to grow very fast. But thank God, we had experiences when we were 14 and 15, such as tasting with him and taking wine trips and tasting in other countries and with other producers . . .

"I think that parents—and I'm a mother-it's important to teach the culture of wine, not only what is in the glass, but the gardening, the taking care of your land, people that are trained and do their job. Every year is not the same. You must build upon your job-not repeating something, modify what you do. It's easy to say, but not easy to make it happen.

"Barbera represents the beauty and the generosity. The second most planted grape in Piemonte-the first is Moscato. Barbera pleases the farmer. It is robust. It has very good quality from the beginning when you plant. The roots are looking for minerals and water.

"I think of the immigrants that moved to Argentina and

other places, the vines they brought with them were Barbera, becoming Bonarda or something.

"It's a red wine that pleases the farmer. It can be feminine as a wine. But it can also be masculine, more power, more extract, a little bit more reserve.

"Something that I love in wine is that it's never the same, everything is a challenge. Barbera, compared to other grapes in Piemonte, is the one that allows you to more of an artist in a way; like an artist, it's very versatile.

"It's about the method of vinification, but it's about the versatility of Barbera that leads it to growing in a different terroir and be an expression of that terroir. You find in Castelnuovo Calcea, Barbera that has more of a pepper note, while in Agliano Terme, more of a smoked note. Each village also expresses terroir in its own way, but maybe compared to Barolo, more easy.

"Sometimes it's not taken as seriously as other reds because of this female roundness that pleases the consumers. Today, Barbera has become popular on wine lists, but a lot has to be done. It's the most widely cultivated red grape in Piemonte, so there is a multitude of Barbera. But there are more and more producers that have understood that Barbera is a grape that a larger number of consumers can understand."

Do you like the comparisons to Barolo and Barbaresco or would you rather not be compared to those wines?

"No, I don't mind, why not the comparison? Barbera is a wine that Giacomo Bologna surprised with Bricco dell'Uccellone by making a Barbera meant to age, and not necessarily young, but with the ability to last longer.

"Maybe it will sound like a spot, an advertisement, but if Nebbiolo is the King of Piemonte wines, then Barbera is the queen. This is what I like to represent with Barbera today.

"We do this job mainly for love, for passion. It's a bit of a fairy tale for our family. Every story starts "once upon a time in this village" . . . *c'era una volta*. We learned from our father; it was a passionate story. Life is harder, but we also have to look to the good stories. So for me Barbera represents this side of the story."

Christoph Kunzli, Le Piane, Boca

Christoph Kunzli was born in Switzerland and over numerous years in the wine business, was able to taste many great Italian wines. One of his favorites was "Campo delle Piane" of Antonio Cerri, a red wine from the Boca zone in Alto Piemonte, not far from Gattinara. He loved this expression of Nebbiolo with small percentages of Vespolina and tasted older vintages from the 1970s with proprietor Cerri. When Cerri became too ill to continue work

Christoph Kunzli

in his vineyards, Kunzli convinced Cerri's family that he would care for the estate with the same attention; he purchased the vineyards and remaining inventory in the mid 1990s and has been producing wines at Le Piane ever since. The portfolio includes Boca DOC along with two or three other red wines that contain Nebbiolo along with Vespolina and Croatina, which are made in a more approachable style than his signature Boca that is meant for long term cellaring.

Boca is made from Nebbiolo, but you do not like to compare your wine with Barolo, correct?

"We should never say we are like Barolo and Barbaresco, because we are very different. Boca, Gattinara and Lessona (the latter two, also Nebbiolo-based wines from Alto Piemonte) have a very strong identity. The only problem is the years of collapse of these regions.

The Wines and Foods of Piemonte

"The self-confidence of the people of these regions was lost. And then the economic situation of Barolo created more of a problem for them. It's strange that when I have discussions with my colleagues, most of them ask me, 'why did you come to Boca?' And I tell them, why not?'"

"Then they say, 'our region is so difficult to understand.' I feel immediately they are trying to tell me that if we were in Barolo, we would be successful. Then I tell them, I came to Boca because I really 'chose' Boca.

"I would never have gone to Barolo, and from Switzerland there is Boca in between. I could see from the former owner that there is great potential here in Boca. I'm not going to say there is greater potential, but we are in the historically old and famous Nebbiolo regions of Piemonte. Gattinara, Lessona and Boca have much longer history than Barolo.

"They ask again, 'You came to Boca. Why didn't you go to Barolo? You're Swiss and you have a lot of money.' They always think the Swiss have a lot of money, which is not always the case!

"But they tell me, 'with money, you could go to Barolo and make great wine.' I tell them no, I want to make wine here, because as we have the best conditions here, it's no problem.

"We have not to be afraid of these wines. We have only to do at least the work of what they do in the vineyards and cellars of Barolo.

"I ask my colleagues, 'are you working well in the vineyards?' They say, 'of course'. I ask them, 'Have you been to the vineyards in Barolo?' They say no and that's the problem. There isn't enough competition in this area. Travaglini (from Gattinara) and some others, of course, know the other wines, but not everybody does.

"The problem is that my colleagues here don't really believe in this region and that's the main point. If you don't believe, why are you making wine here?

"They see my passion for this region. For me, Boca is a wine I like very much and yes, I chose this wine. They think I'm a little bit crazy. They don't get the idea. So after all this time, they should get the idea that my wine is something special and they should be motivated to do something better.

"I have always been clear on these things in this region. No, we are not a copy of Barolo. We are the original Nebbiolo, but we forgot it. We existed in Piemonte before Barolo.

"Everytime when you go through our region, you get this very bad feeling, 'we are less than Barolo.' So for these people, there's no chance. For them, Barolo is rich and we are poor.

I always tell them, we need the passion. In the 1930s, there were 40,000 hectares here. Every family, everbody lived from wine-producing. Everything was wine here.

But then in the 1950s, the old economic system collapsed. Eventually the people that remained in this business were the poor. 'Oh, you still make wine.'

"My case is very unusual for this region, that someone from Switzerland came here to make wine. They wonder why I do this.

"What's strange though is that even after all the awards we've garnered in all these years, they still have doubts about this region. They still think that if they were in Barolo, they'd be rich. But this is not necessarily true. If you work bad in Barolo like you work here sometimes, you'd be nobody!

"I am super critical on this subject, but that's because I have a clear idea of what I want to do. In my view, I could have never made Nebbiolo-wines with barrique. Why do you do it? Because of the market.

"A lot of producers went to barrique, but now they have scaled back and use large casks. This to me shows a lack of character, in a way.

"I go to Burgundy to taste wines from producers I like a lot. I learn a lot of things this way. I think in terms of maturing a wine and producing one that is true to its origins. The French have a bit more discipline in this. Maybe they are a bit stubborn, maybe they are a bit dull sometimes, but it's not possible to change Romanée Conti or Comte de Vogüé Musigny. When you go into these cellars, you understand what you have to do—no compromise.

"Do what you think is right for your wines—and that's it. These producers that change their practices in the cellar—it's for the market. It's not great wine. Maybe they don't know what they want to do.

"I've tasted so many great wines in the world, so for me, great wine is great wine. I found my style looking to old producing methods. It doesn't bother me what someone tells me. I know what I want to do. I do what I want to do. For me, the style for our wines was always clear—big barrels, long aging, time.

"Wine is something that takes you somewhere-there should be emotion. If someone doesn't like your wine, that's OK. You can't make the wine for everyone. You have to make your own wine and there are enough people in the world that will appreciate that wine.

"For Boca, it's difficult anyway as we are still unknown as a region, so why not make a wine of strong character?"

Cinzia Travaglini, Gattinara

Cinzia Travaglini and her husband Massimo Collauto are the proprietors of the great Gattinara estate, Travaglini. Of the 100 hectares in the approved production zone, Travaglini owns 60, making them *the* reference point for this great Alto Piemonte red.

Please tell me about your family's history here in Gattinara.

"Ours is a very historic cellar, one that was begun with the production of wines by my father in 1958. His grandfather and grandmother first grew grapes in the mid 19th century. My husband Massimo is the fourth generation—he controls production."

Everyone knows Barolo and Barbaresco, but Gattinara is not as famous, despite the fact that it is also produced from Nebbiolo. How do you compare these wines?

"The difference between Gattinara and the wines of Barolo and Barbaresco have to do with soil and microclimate. We have a very windy, dry climate. We have breezes that flow in between the hills, which are important for the aromatic qualities of the wine and for the cleanliness of the grapes. Many of the vineyards of Barolo and Barbaresco are planted on hillsides that are protected from the winds.

"The soil is very old, of the Monte Rosa and Alps. There are elements of porphyr, clay which are found in the wine. The wines are silky and elegant."

How do you sell Gattinara?

"The biggest market in is our area. In Italy, in the last ten years, we are now selling a little more, as people are now starting to recognize the wines from northern Piemonte. It is Nebbiolo, a very, elegant, fine wine, one that is easy to drink with food."

When you sell it, do you compare it with Barolo and Barbaresco or do you not try to do that?

"No, no we do it all the time. There are differences in soil and weather. Maybe Barolo and Barbaresco are more complex or perhaps I should say more masculine. But Gattinara in particular among the Nebbiolo-based wines of northern Piemonte, is very elegant. The soil here is rocky, which gives us a lot of minerality. There is great temperature excursion here; it's possible to have 26 or 27 degrees during the day, but at night, 10 degrees. This is very important for the perfume and elegance of the wine."

Would you say that Gattinara can age as well as Barolo and Barbaresco?

"Yes, Gattinara has a long life. If you keep the wines in good shape, you can keep the wines for 20, 30 even 50 years. We recently opened a magnum of 1967 Gattinara and it showed great freshness and plenty of life—it was a beautiful experience."

What is the best experience you have here making the wines?

"We know that more young people start to understand Nebbiolo, because Nebbiolo is very fine wine. You start to love Nebbiolo and it's very difficult to come back. In the future, this will become a more and more important area."

PART THREE

Interviews with Chefs

Manuel Bouchard, Antinè, Barbaresco

Manuel Bouchard, born in 1988, has been the chef/proprietor at Antinè in the town of Barbaresco since 2013. This is the first restaurant he has owned, although he has been cooking for many years, learning his trade from such celebrated chefs as Marco Sacco, Antonio Cannavacciuolo, Stefano Ciotti and Sergio Oddovero. He notes that while he has always had a great passion for cooking, it was these individuals that instilled discipline in him, allowing him to take on new challenges and constantly fuel his desire for his talent and enthusiasm.

In a zone with great red wines, do you feel obliged to feature classic pairings with these wines?

"Yes, I have to say that we have the good fortune to have a restaurant in the little historic center of a country town such as Barbaresco that is famous for its wine throughout the world. Over the years in fact, we have have the good fortune to have many visitors from each part of the globe that stopped for a day or more to taste this great wine, either at the Enoteca Regionale or directly at the cellars together with the producers and often wanted to taste these wines with the plates I prepared at the restaurant. It is an enormous satisfaction to see how the proper dishes are assembled and served with these great wines."

What would you serve with a young Barbaresco and what would you pair with an older Barbaresco, say at least ten years old?

"With a young Barbaresco, one can sample different plates: from light antipasti such as vitello tonnato, carne cruda and why not, seared scallops resembling a modern *giardiniera*. For first courses, one can also try my raviolini (the traditional plin), traditional tajarin of butter and *tartufi bianchi* (when the season permits), *gnocchi di patate* with snails in lard and clams, spaghetti *trafilato al bronzo* (a roughly filled spaghetti) with leeks and *salsiccia di Bra* (veal sausage from Bra), etc.

"However with an older wine, we would go directly to the main courses in a manner that can be comforting to me and to the client.

"With a wine that has aged for more than ten years, I can slot in *guanciale* (cheek) of Piemontese beef with a Barbaresco reduction, accompanied by a purée of potatoes and mustard. Another idea can be my *sottofiletto* of beef served with a sauce of marrow and with a breaded Krapfen in *tartufi neri* and fonduta. Another idea can be Rolata of rabbit served with peppers, a cube of potato purée and lemon and a chutney of pepperoni."

Are there pairings for Barbaresco or other local reds, such as Barbera or Dolcetto that can be considered uncharacteristic or surpising?

"Yes, absolutely, often when we taste a red wine, be it a Barbera, a Barbaresco or a Dolcetto with fish or perhaps with chocolate, we find ourselves a little wrong-footed and we sometimes consider a pairing a little uncharacteristic. But over the years with the help of producers and from great chefs that often look for certain ways of educating us about wine and food, we have discovered from the pairings truly uncommon ones that, if we can say with certainty we considered surprising!"

Are there courses that you serve especially in the winter or in the summer?

"Yes, absolutely, our restaurant changes its plates constantly during the year. These changes happen because of the changes of the seasons and also because of the differences of the available materials.

"In my plates, we always have seasonal vegetables and naturally each time that there is a specific ingredient that is not in season, I change the plate and update it with a new one, always making use of the most peak materials at that time. For me, it is fundamental that my clients are tasting in the courses I have created the freshness of a vegetable or whatever other ingredient that was picked because it was seasonal. No method of long-term conservation of any type of vegetable is used in my kitchen. According to me, the dish would not be the same!"

Massimo Corso, Osteria Veglio, La Morra / LALIBERA, Alba

Massimo Corso is one of the Langhe's most innovative chefs. He arrived at LALIBERA in the ancient center of Alba in 2005, and served as executive chef here for nine years.

He recently left LALIBERA to become chef and partner at Osteria Veglio in La Morra. This interview with Corso was conducted at LALIBERA in 2014.

Massimo Corso

How do you gain publicity for the restaurant?

"It's always been a case of word-of-mouth. It's very important to get customers to return year after year. This is fundamental."

*Are there special pairings of food and wine you work with
at the restaurant?*

"I think that with *capretto* (goat), one should drink a simple wine.
For more important dishes such as veal or *brasato*, this is the occasion for a great wine such as Barolo or Barbaresco; these wines
also work well with *tartufo bianco*. This is ideal with a great red
wine in October and especially in November and December."

*What ingredients, what plates would you serve in winter and which
would you serve in summer?*

"As you know, our cuisine is very essential, based on seasonal
products of the highest quality and cooked simply to make the
most of them to the maximum.

"In winter, as a primo, we have *salsiccia di Bra, porri de Cervere*
(leeks from Cervere in Cuneo), potatoes and pecorino suffed in a la-
sagna or genuine polpo with broccoli as a condiment to the linguine
"Pastificio Mancini", a takeoff on the classic *tajarin al ragu.*

"As a second, always in wintertime, we serve boiled *gallina*
(an older hen) with cooked thistles in broth and the traditional
sauces (green, red and giardinera), milk-fed lamb roasted in
thyme with arichokes of Albegna, cooked tripe in umido (stew)
and then cooked with cheese in the oven with pistachios or pigeon with endive grilled and beetroot.

"In summer, the cuisine is lighter allowing for fresher and
more delicate flavors.

"As a *primo*, we serve the traditional ravioli *"Seirass del fin"*
(typical fresh ricotta) with *burro d'alpeggio* (mountain butter),
zucchette trombette with candied baccalà and Taggiasche olives or
reginette with ragù of summer vegetables and strong Bra.

"For a *secondo, scamone* (rump) of veal cooked rare and
served cold with beans and tomatoes, cutlet of *sanato* (milk-fed
veal) *alla milanese* with porcini mushrooms, a small carp mixed
or guinea flow roasted with herbs and potatoes and tomatoes.
Our cuisine takes its inspiration from tradition but above all
from the best products we can acquire at the moment.

"Another important thing is the 360-degree comparison of among all the staff of the resturant, sharing ideas, impressions, small flashes that come always during discussions; this results in obtaining pleasant surprises such as our *linguine "pastificio Mancini."*

"We certainly remain innovative in our field and the confrontation with other colleagues is fundamental. I love always going to the restaurant and discovering plates of colleagues near us; it is fascinating and opens one's mind as far as utilizing enormously the potential that each single ingredient should have."

Enrico Crippa, Piazza Duomo, Alba

Enrico Crippa, born in the neighboring region of Lombardia in 1971, has worked at several of Europe's finest restaurants, including Ledoyen in Paris, Buerheisel in Strasbourg and El Bulli in Roses, Spain. In 1996, he opened Gualtiero Marchesi's restaurant in Kobe, Japan and spent three years there, perfecting his craft. After relocating to Italy, he met with the Ceretto family, one of Piemonte's greatest producers of Barolo and Barbaresco; in 2005, Bruno Ceretto opened Piazza Duomo with Crippa as executive chef. The restaurant was awarded its first Michelin-star in 2006, its second in 2009 and in November, 2012, it was awarded a third Michelin star. In April 2015, Piazza Duomo was ranked as #27 on a list of the 50 Best Restaurants in the World.

Enrico Crippa

This is not a very traditional restaurant or cuisine for Alba. What was the reaction when you first opened?

"In the beginning, the locals were looking to La Piola (the osteria situated directly below Piazza Duomo) for simple, traditional cuisine. Once they had discovered that and were pleased, the next step was to discover the cuisine upstairs.

"It's always been the research for us in the seasonality, in the flavors. We thought that we had the type of cuisine that had created itself. It's taking our cuisine to a new level while keeping it very fresh and always with an eye on the soil, the land.

"People discovered this cuisine, which was very different from La Piola. They became to understand this, step by step, year by year. We started to achieve recognition, but more than that, people started to understand what we tried to do."

From where do you get your inspiration?

"There's not really one moment. There could be a dark moment and then there are moments when you are inspired. The vegetable garden is my main inspiration.

I can get my inspiration by taking a walk or by looking at a picture—there is not a precise scheme."

Tell me about this garden.

"We found this land, just before you enter Barolo and there was nothing there. So we started to cultivate and made everything biological.

"We added more old herbs and edible flowers. But I always tried to stay true to the tradition of seasonal Italian vegetables and fruit and now we have asparagus and strawberries.

"This is important for us, as many people have stopped eating meat, as they stick with vegetables and fish.

"Having this vegetable garden is an advantage because the vegetables are always fresh as there's no problem with transportation on trucks, as we can always receive them fresh. The colors of the vegetable are true, when it's green, it's green, when it's red, it's red.

The freshness and the flavors are consistent and un-equaled. The customers appreciate the freshness; eating vegetables that have been taken from the garden just three hours earlier is totally different than eating vegetables from the market. For us, it's very, very important to have this aspect"

Now that you have received your third Michelin star and are now ranked among the top 30 restaurants in the world, what is your objective? How do you improve? How do you stay concentrated on being the best chef and making this the best restaurant you can?

"The objective is to remain on as well as climb the list of the 50 Best Restaurants, looking continually to be the best and certainly sustaining this level, which is a daily effort of maintaining our philosophy of cuisine and service."

Partial list of plates offered regularly during winter:

CARDO GOBBO E LA SUA SALSA

CREMA DI PATATE E LAPSANG SOUCHONG,
   TARTUFO BIANCO D'ALBA

RISOTTO FUNGHI PORCINI E ANICE STELLATO

ANIMELLE E CARCIOFI

Partial list of plates offered regularly during summer:

GAMBERO DI SANREMO, CILIEGIA E POMODORO

CARNE CRUDA DI VITELLO E FRAGOLE

ZUPPA DI PEPERONI DI SENISE

GOURMANDISE DI CILIEGIE

Luca Fassone, L'Angolo di Rosina, Novello

Luca Fassone was born in the town of Bra, in the province of Cuneo in 1972. He has been the chef at L'Angolo di Rosina for the past six years. Previous to this, he worked for twenty years at Ristorante Belvedere in La Morra.

Luca Fassone

I think that your tajarin is exceptional. Do you have a secret? Tell me about the tradition of tajarin in the Langhe.

"For the *tajarin*, it's not a secret. We use prime, excellent ingredients, with a recipe that I refined over many years of work. I use biological flour from the mill Sobrino of La Morra and high quality egg yolks, while for the sauce, a good foundation of vegetables, with a blend of pork, veal and other sausages; also I use tomatoes that I prefer. I cook this for five hours. To complete this work, I briefly cook the tajarin in water with salt, finishing in a frying pan with the highest quality butter, sauce and fresh rosemary."

In a zone famous for its great red wines, do you feel obliged to pair traditional local foods with this wines?

"I'm not obliged, but I do see the fortune that we have living here, being able to use our wines in a natural way. In our zone, it's easy to pair our plates with the local wines, because it is an age-old tradition. We have ample choices of recipes, from very rich to very lean, acidic or less acidic, just as we have an ample selection of various wines.

The Wines and Foods of Piemonte

We also have recipes that include wine, that require a similar accompanying wine."

What dishes would you pair with a young Barbaresco or Barolo?
What about with an older Barbaresco or Barolo?

"For a young Barbaresco or Barolo, I can match with dishes that
are of a strong and intense flavor, preferring meat, such as rabbit,
roasted veal or pork. For an older example of these wines, we
would certainly match them with plates of a decisive flavor, beef
stews or dishes of game, hare, wild boar and goat."

Are there wine pairings that you have seen that you considered out of
the ordinary or a surprise?

"I noticed the strange tendency to referigerate wines that ought
to be served around 20 degrees C (65 degrees F) and serve them
not only with meats, but also throughout the meal. I have also
seen Moscato served as an aperitif."

Are there dishes that you serve in the winter or in the summer that
are tailored for these seasons?

"First, understand that there are dishes on our menu that are
served all year round and do not change; these include *tajarin*,
carne cruda, vitello tonnato, etc.

"Other plates follow the seasons, such as certain vegetables,
like asparagus and mushrooms, or thistles, leeks, and the white
truffles from Alba.

"Others follow the temperatures, such as cold appetizers
that are preferred in the summer, while fondue, game, *bagna*
cauda and polenta are definitely dishes for the colder seasons."

Dario Marini, Il Fierobecco, Maggiora

Dario Marini, born in 1974, first worked in a kitchen at the age
of 14, cultivating his great passion for food. In 2014, he became
chef at Il Fierobecco, a small restaurant in the town of Maggiora, in the heart of Alto Piemonte. He says his work there is, in

some ways, "to create a contest among the local wines, vineyards and producers."

Tell me about your education in fine cuisine.

"I had the honor of learning from great chefs that did not appear on television to romanticize and make public this occupation that can be a balance between stealing secrets and having a sense of duty and respect for the hierarchy. Now it seems like this is work for everyone, but that clearly is not so!"

Tell me about Alto Piemonte and how you link the local foods and wines?

"This is a zone of recently rediscovered great wines, but in truth, our culture and our history permit a reevaluation of our territory also from a culinary point of view, notwithstanding that Alto Piemonte does not possess the typical indigenous gastronomy as strong as the influence of the Lombardians.

"However, one can create with a maginificent Nebbiolo plates from Alto Piemonte using the great basic materials that are offered throughout Piemonte and all of Italy. Sublime meats such as fassona, cheeses, truffles, hazelnuts and then the cultivated wines; together the structure of the plate gives a beginning to new recipes, revisiting and reworking to heighten the emotions.

"Or you can dare, to risk sugesting Nebbiolo within the plates like making a tortelli pasta with Nebbiolo with a stuffed pigeon . . . or making a risotto with hazelnuts and a reduction of Boca and, why not, inventing a plate such as a salad of calamari with rabbit and *puntarelle* (chicory) and drink a good glass of Maggiorina!

"There are a thousand possibilities, especially with wines that are versatile. But the thing that I would add is that the basic excellent materials make the difference . . . thus a piece of alpeggio cheese, with bread with a glass of Le Piane in their simplest authenticity, giving great emotions . . . and it is here that my work is exalted in these sensory marriages!"

How do the seasons affect your cuisine?

"The seasons have and should have a strong influence on the composition of the plates as the natural raw materials are the fruit of the seasons, so using an orange in August is scandalous!

In this age, where every product could be available at whatever moment I choose to use them, I opt for only the freshest ingredients of the season, whenever possible available from the farmer or the producer, checking the quality, the authenticity and naturalness of the product!"

How would you define your cooking? From where do you get your inspiration?

"I would define my cuisine 'without compromises', respecting perhaps my character. The concept of correct and incorrect, what you can do and should do—that makes the difference!

"I think that my inspiration derives in the first place as a wish to experiment (better with the plates than words!) and in the second place, from the alchemy of my family where the complicity and the sharing of this passion with my wife Michela has spurred us and dared us to always believe!"

Barbara Pastura

Barbara Pastura is the sister of Massimo Pastura, propietor of Cascina La Ghersa, a producer known for his Barbera d'Asti from the Nizza district. Barbara was born in 1974 and started to work at age fourteen when she attended the hotel-management school of Agliano Terme, near the city of Asti. She eventually moved on to work in the kitchens of several restaurants in the Langhe and Monferrato. In 2013, she became the owner and chef of The B, a charming *ristorante* with a lovely view of the Nizza Monferrato countryside. The restaurant is now closed, but before this took place, I interviewed Barbara after dinner one evening.

In a zone with great red wines, do you feel obliged to feature classic pairings with these wines?

"Everything depends on which type of cuisine each restaurant wants to propose. I try to stay on this territory, suggesting the specialties of our tradition in a modern touch, with lighter cooking and with fresh and seasonal ingredients. In this way, all the served dishes are surely suitable with these important red wines, but also the local white wines."

Your area specializes in the production of Barbera. What are your favorite food pairings with Barbera (perhaps something specific on your menu)?

"The local cuisine offers different combinations with Barbera wine; indeed it was born to go with these wines. My favorite proposals, present in our menu, are risotto Canaroli with local sausage and Barbera; also the Fassone (our typical veal meat) stew cooked in Barbera."

Are there courses you serve specifically in the summer or winter? What ingredients are you specifically able to use in the summer, but not winter?

"I use fresh and local raw materials, so linked to the seasonal products. During the summer my cuisine is fresher with seasonal vegetables like zucchini, eggplant and peppers, while during the winter, I use Savoy cabbage, cauliflowers, fennel and our famous *cardo gobbo* (a particular thistle that grows only in this area). Even the meats are prepared with lighter cooking during the summer like salted Fassone *scamone* (a particular part of Fassone veal), while during the winter, there is longer preparation such as braised and stewed meats cooked in Barbera or Barolo."

Please tell me about tartufi bianchi. Can you briefly describe their characteristics and how they are used at your restaurant?

"For me, the white truffle is like the gold of Langhe and Monferrato, given its intense aroma, which fills the restaurant and starts to satisfy our senses.

The Wines and Foods of Piemonte

"Being in the white truffle area during the season, from the middle of September until December, we propose and serve them in combination with the most suitable courses, like the famous *tagliolini* (*tajarin*), Fassone raw meat, creamy risotto with our most important cheeses (Raschera, Toma Piemontese, Robiola of Roc-caverano, etc.) with fried egg or the "trifulau" coquette composed of soft polenta, yolks, fondues and truffle flakes on tops.

"For people who are most curious about new combinations, please don't miss a good vanilla ice cream with truffle on top!"

Luca Pellegrino, Ristorante Le Torri, Castiglione Falletto

Luca Pellgrino, born in Cu-neo, has enjoyed a wide variety of experiences as a chef, from his time in the military to his work at Tre Verghe d'Oro in Pradleves. He has been the chef at Le Torri since 2013; his wife Luisa is co-proprietor.

Can you tell me about the tradition of tajarin in the Langhe? Am I correct in thinking that this dish is a source of pride for local chefs?

"Tajarin is certainly a typical dish of this zone, one that has been served since the 1400s, as a simple plate for the local population. It was served

Luca Pellegrino

with a sauce of chicken giblets as *finanziera*, another simple dish of the Langhe cuisine, which was also made with such things as rooster crests and veal brains.

"Today tajarin is a plate that I think represents this land to the world, as it is often served with the prized *tartufi bianchi* of

Alba; this is unlike the poor dish it once was, as today, we use thirty brown eggs per one kilogram of flour.

"I think that no matter where you go in the area, each chef has his own recipe for tajarin."

In a zone so famous for its red wines, do you feel obliged to pair these wines with classic local, traditional foods?

"I think that the good fortune of being a chef and restaurateur in this area is directly linked to the wines. In the first place, certainly these great wines have been responsible for a large influx in tourism, as the producers have been able to exploit their products to the world. Of course, a great glass of wine requires a great dish to accompany it!"

What wines would you serve with a younger as well as an older Barolo or Barbaresco?

"For a relatively young Barolo or Barbaresco, I would pair an egg croquette in a crust of hazelnut with fonduta and truffle. For an older example of these wines, cheek of braised *fassona* (Piemontese beef) or for something simpler, an assortment of aged cheeses."

Can you give me an example of an unusual pairing with a local red wine?

"A fairly unusual combination would be salmon fillet with a Barolo."

Are there dishes you serve according to the seasons, be it winter or summer?

"Certainly for my cuisine, I think about following the seasons of the products, as do my colleagues. In the fall, we offer dishes with mushrooms and truffles, as well as dishes such as *baccala* served with *bagna cauda* (a Piemontese sauce with garlic, anchovies and oil) that in the spring and summer would be a bit heavy."

Two Hundred-Plus Highly Recommended
Wines from Piemonte

Sparkling

Enrico Serafino Alta Langa Brut "Zero"

Ettore Germano Alta Langa Brut

Fontanafredda Alta Langa Brut "Vigna Gatinera"

Banfi Alta Langa "Cuvée Aurora" Rosé

Cocchi Alta Langa "Pas Dosé" Brut Nature

Bruno Giacosa Brut

Cuvage Brut Rosé

Cascina Chicco Brut

Borgo Maragliano Brut Riserva "Giuseppe Galliano"

Erpacrife

Rocche del Manzoni "Valentino Riserva Elena"

Cascina Chicco "Cuvée Zero"

Deltetto Brut Rosé

Cieck Erbaluce di Caluso Spumante "San Giorgio"

Barbaglia Uva Rara Brut

Romano Dogliotti Asti Spumante "La Caudrina"

Ca' D'Gal Moscato d'Asti "Vigne Vecchie"

Enrico Serafino Moscato d'Asti (Black Bottle)

Fontanafredda Moscato d'Asti "Moncucco"

Saracco "Moscato d'Autunno"

Forteto della Luja Moscato d'Asti "Piasa San Maurizio"

Braida Moscato d'Asti "Vigna Senza Nome"

La Spinetta Moscato d'Asti "Biancospino"

Scagliola Moscato d'Asti "Volo di Farfalle"

Braida Brachetto d'Acqui

Marenco Brachetto d'Acqui "Pineto"

Il Falchetto Brachetto d'Acqui

Cavallero Brachetto d'Acqui

Marco Porello Birbet
Elio Perrone "Bigarò"

White

Angelo Negro Roero Arneis "Perdaudin"
Matteo Correggia Roero Arneis
Marco Porello Roero Arneis "Camestri"
Malabaila Roero Arneis "Pradvaj"
Malvirà Roero Arneis "Saglietto"
Malvirà Roero Arneis "Trinità"
Monchiero Carbone Roero Arneis "Cecu d'la Biunda"
Cornarea Roero Arneis Enritard
Bruno Giacosa Roero Arneis
Ghiomo Langhe Arneis "Imprimis"
Gianni Voerzio Langhe Arneis "Bricco Capellina"
Broglia Gavi "Bruno Broglia"
Castello di Tassarolo Gavi "Alborina"
Castellari Bergaglio Gavi "Fornaci"
Castellari Bergaglio Gavi "Pilin"
Nicola Bergaglio Gavi "Minaia"
Villa Sparina Gavi
La Ghibellina Gavi di Gavi "Mainìn"
Angelo Negro Langhe Favorita "Onorata"
Marco Porello Langhe Favorita
Vigne Marina Coppi Colli Tortonesi Favorita "Marine"
Ettore Germano Riesling "Herzu"
G.D. Vajra Riesling "Pètracine"
Elvio Cogno Anas Cëtta
Le Strette Nas-cëtta
Orsolani Erbaluce di Caluso "La Rustia"
Orsolani Erbaluce di Caluso "Vignot S. Antonio"
Cieck Erbaluce di Caluso "Misobolo"
La Campore Erbaluce di Caluso
Vigne Marina Coppi Timorasso "Fausto"
Vigneti Massa Timorasso "Sterpi"
Luigi Boveri Filari di Timorasso

The Wines and Foods of Piemonte

Paolo Scavino Barolo "Bricco Ambrogio"

Red

Barolo Mascarello Barolo
Giuseppe Rinaldi Barolo "Tre Tini"
Elio Grasso Barolo "Gavarini Chiniera"
Massolino Barolo "Parussi"
Massolino Barolo Riserva "Vigna Rionda"
Borgogno Barolo Riserva
G.D. Vajra Barolo "Bricco delle Viole"
Mario Marengo Barolo "Bricco delle Viole"
Paolo Scavino Barolo "Bricco Ambrogio"
Paolo Scavino Barolo Rocche dell'Annunziata Riserva
Francesco Rinaldi Barolo "Brunate"
Francesco Rinaldo Barolo "Cannubi"
Serio e Battista Borgogno Barolo "Cannubi"
Cantina del Nebbiolo Barolo "Cannubi Boschis"
Luigi Einaudi Barolo "Terlo—Vigna Coste Grimaldi"
Vietti Barolo "Rocche di Castiglione"
Renato Ratti Barolo "Conca"
Renato Ratti Barolo "Rocche dell' Annunziata"

Roberto Voerzio Barolo "Brunate"

Roberto Voerzio Barolo "La Serra"

Marcarini Barolo "Brunate"

E. Molino Barolo "Bricco Rocca"

Cavallotto Barolo "Bricco Boschis—Riserva San Giuseppe"

Cordero di Montezemolo Barolo "Enrico VI"

Giacomo Fenocchio Barolo "Villero"

E. Mirafiore Barolo "Lazzarito"

Vietti Barolo "Lazzarito"

Ettore Germano Barolo "Prapò"

Ceretto Barolo "Prapò"

Mauro Sebaste Barolo "Prapò"

Umberto Fracassi Barolo

Giovanni Rosso Barolo "Ceretta"

Paolo Manzone Barolo "Meriame"

Poderi Oddero Barolo "Bussia Soprana—Vigna Mondoca"

Michele Chiarlo Barolo "Cerequio"

Elvio Cogno Barolo "Vigna Elena"

Elvio Cogno Barolo "Bricco Pernice"

Batasiolo Barolo "Boscareto"

Aldo Conterno Barolo "Gran Bussia"

Bruno Giacosa Barolo Riserva "Le Rocche del Falletto"

Pio Cesare Barolo "Ornato"

Giacomo Conterno Barolo "Monfortino"

Rocche Costamagna Barolo Riserva "Bricco Francesco"

Burlotto Barolo "Monvigliero"

Fratelli Alessandria Barolo "Monvigliero"

Castello di Verduno Barolo Riserva "Monvigliero"

Rattalino Barolo "Trentaquattro 34"

Umberto Fracassi Barolo

Conterno Fantino Barolo "Sori Ginestra"

Giovanni Manzone Barolo Riserva "Gramolere"

Gillardi Barolo

Cascina delle Rose Barbaresco "Rio Sordo"

Produttori del Barbaresco "Montestefano"

Rizzi Barbaresco "Boito"

Bottle and glass of Castello di Verduno Barolo "Monvigliero" Riserva

Elvio Pertinace Barbaresco "Nervo"

Rattalino Barbaresco "Quarantadue 42"

Fiorenzo Nada Barbaresco "Rombone"

Fontanabianca Barbaresco "Sori Burdin"

Bruno Giacosa Barbaresco Riserva "Asili"

Marchesi di Grésy Barbaresco "Camp Gros"

Ceretto Barbaresco "Asili"

Serafino Rivella Barbaresco "Montestefano"

Ada Nada Barbaresco "Elisa"

Albino Rocca Barbaresco "Montersino"

Angelo Negro Roero Riserva "Sadisfà"

Pelassa Roero Riserva "Antaniolo"

Matteo Correggia Roero Riserva "Rocche d'Ampsej"

Marco Porello Roero "Torretta"

Enrico Serafino Roero "Pasiunà"

Gaja "Sori San Lorenzo"

Cascina delle Rose Langhe Nebbiolo

Mario Marengo Nebbiolo d'Alba

Gabriele Scaglione Langhe Rosso "Tutto Dipende da dove Vuoi
    Andare"

Chionetti Dolcetto di Dogliani "San Luigi"

San Fereolo Dogliani Superiore

Anna Maria Abbona Dogliani Superiore "San Bernardo"

Pecchenino Dogliani Superiore "Bricco Botti"

Gillardi Dogliani Superiore "Cursalet"

Clavesana Dogliani Superiore "587"

Giovanni Prandi Dolcetto di Diano d'Alba "Sörì Colombè"

Claudio Alario Dolcetto di Diano d'Alba "Montagrillo"

Fontanafredda Dolcetto di Diano d'Alba "La Lepre"

Marcarini Dolcetto d'Alba "Boschi di Berri"

Cascina Roccalini Dolcetto d'Alba

Pio Cesare Dolcetto d'Alba

Giuseppe Mascarello Dolcetto d'Alba "Santo Stefano di Perno"

Rocche Costamagna Dolcetto d'Alba "Rubis"

Cascina Boccaccio Ovada Riserva "Nonno Rucchein"

Cascina La Ghersa Barbera d'Asti Superiore Nizza "Vignassa"

Michele Chiarlo Barbera d'Asti Superiore Nizza "La Court"
L'Armangia Barbera d'Asti Superiore Nizza "Vignali"
Guido Berta Barbera d'Asti Superiore Nizza "Canto di Luna"
Armando Chiappone Barbera d'Asti Superiore Nizza "Ru"
Tenuta Garetto Barbera d'Asti Superiore Nizza "Favà"
Tenuta Garetto Barbera d'Asti "Tra Neuit e Dì"
Bersano Barbera d'Asti "Costalunga"
Braida Barbera d'Asti "Bricco dell'Uccellone"
Bel-Sit Barbera d'Asti Superiore "Sichivej"
Giuseppe Bocchino Barbera d'Asti "Blincin"
Vietti Barbera d'Alba "Scarrone Vigna Vecchia"
Pio Cesare Barbera d'Alba "Fides"
Elio Grasso Barbera d'Alba "Vigna Martina"
Monchiero Carbone Barbera d'Alba "Mon Birone"
Castello di Tassarolo Barbera "Titouan" (Piemonte)
Vigne Marina Coppi Colline Tortonesi Barbera Superiore
    "I Grop"
Cascina la Ghersa Colli Tortonesi Croatina "Smenta"
Accornero Grignolino del Monferrato Casalese "Bricco del Bosco
    Vigne Vecchie"
Pierino Vellano Grignolino del Monferrato Casalese "Osiri"
Braida Grignolino d'Asti "Limone"
Marco Crivelli Grignolino d'Asti
Gaudio Grignolino del Monferrato "Bricco Mondalino"
Montalbera Ruché di Castagnole Monferrato "Laccento"
Dacapo Ruché di Castagnole Monferrato "Majoli"
Cantine Sant'Agata Ruché di Castagnole Monferrato "'Na Vota"
Marco Crivelli Ruché di Castagnole Monferrato
Balbiano Freisa di Chieri "Vigna della Regina"
Balbiano Freisa di Chieri "Surpreisa"
G.D. Vajra Freisa "Kye'" (Langhe)
Giuseppe Mascarello Freisa "Toetto" (Langhe)
Luigi Giordano Freisa (Langhe)
Burlotto Pelaverga
Castello di Verduno Pelaverga "Bellis Perennis"
Fratelli Alessandria Pelaverga "Speziale"

Poderi Colla Langhe Rosso "Bricco del Drago"
Podere Ruggieri Corsini Langhe Rosso Albarossa
Le Piane Boca
Le Piane "Maggiorina"
Le Piane "Le Piane"
Barbaglia Boca
Travaglini Gattinara Riserva
Antoniolo Gattinara "Osso San Grato"
Rovelloti Gattinara Riserva "Costa del Salmino"
Luca Caligaris Gattinara
Paride Iaretti Gattinara
Vallana Gattinara
Cantalupo Ghemme "Collis Breclamae"
Francesco Brigatti Ghemme "Oltre il Bosco"
Mazzoni Ghemme "Ai Livelli"
Mazzoni Colline Novaresi Nebbiolo del Monteregio
Boniperti Colline Novaresi Nebbiolo "CarLiN"
Francesco Brigatti Colline Novaresi Nebbiolo "Mötfrei"
Cantina dei Produttori di Carema Carema "Classico" (black label)
Ferrando Carema "Etichetta Nera"
Cantina Garrone Prünent
Le Pianelle Bramaterra
Tenute Sella Bramaterra
Odilio Antoniotti Bramaterra
La Prevostura Lessona
Proprietà Sperino Coste della Sesia Rosso "Uvaggio"
Noah Coste della Sesia Croatina
Boniperti Fara
Boniperti Vespolina
Francesca Castaldi "Nina" (Colline Novaresi Vespolina)

Rosato

La Prevostura Costa della Sesia Rosato "Corrina"
Le Pianelle "Al Posto dei Fiori"
Luca Caligaris Coste della Sesia "Rosa di Martina"
Proprietà Sperino Costa della Sesia Rosato "Rosa di Rosa"

Agrinova Roccafurà Rosato
Cantina Le Viti Rosato "Briosec"
Burlotto Vio Rosato "Elatis"

Dolci

Cantagal Erbaluce di Caluso Passito
Orsolani Erbaluce di Caluso Passito "Ambra"
Cieck Erbaluce di Caluso Passito "Alladium"
Angelo Negro Roero Arneis Passito
Cornarea Passito di Arneis "Tarasco"
Deltetto "Bric di Lun"
Forteto della Luja Moscato Passito (Loazzolo DOC)
Borgo Maragliano Moscato Passito (Loazzolo DOC)
Olim Bauda Piemonte Moscato Passito "San Giovanni"
Castellari Bergaglio "Gavium" (Naturally Sweet Gavi)
Balbiano Malvasia di Castelnuovo Don Bosco
Balbiano Cari
Marenco Brachetto Passito "Pissrí"
Bragnagnolo Brachetto Passito "Passione"

Barolo Chinato

Cappellano
Rocche Costamagna
Fontanafredda
Marcarini
Marchesi di Barolo
Cordero di Montezemolo

Recommended Restaurants

Organized by province:

Alessandria (AL)
Asti (AT)
Biella (BI)
Cuneo (CN)
Novara (NO)
Torino (TO)
Verbano-Cusio-Ossola (VB)
Vercelli (VC)

And then alphabetically, by town

PROVINCE OF ALESSANDRIA

Osteria della Luna in Brdrodo
Via Legnano, 12
Alessandria (AL)
(39) 0131 231898

Ristorante Duomo
Via Parma, 28
Alessandria (AL)
(39) 0131 52631
www.ristorante-duomo.com

Ristorante Il Grappolo
Via Casale, 28
Alessandria (AL)
(39) 0131 253217
www.ristoranteilgrappolo.it

Locanda dell'Olmo
Piazza Mercato, 6
Bosco Marengo (AL)
(39) 0131 299186
www.bondivini.it

Ristorante Al Cortese
Via Serravalle, 69
Novi Ligure (AL)
(39) 0143 323219
www.alcortese.com

Locanda San Martino
Via Roma, 26
Pasturana (AL)
(39) 0143 58444
www.locandasanmartino.com

Le Cicale
Via Pineroli 32
Spinetta Marengo (AL)
(39) 0131 216130
www.lecicale.net

La Fermata
Via Bolla, 2
Spinetta Marengo (AL)
(39) 0131 617508
www.ristorantelafermata.com

Ristorante Belvedere 1919
Località Pessinate
15060 Cantalupo Ligure (AL)
(39) 0143 93138
www.belvedere1919.it

Peccati di Gola
Via Roma, 19R
Gavi (AL)
(39) 0143 643686
www.peccatidigola.com

PROVINCE OF ASTI

Osteria Lamilonga
Via Cristoforo Colombo, 10
Agliano Terme (AT)
(39) 0141 954089
www.osterialamilonga.it

Ristorante La Gallina
Frazione Monterotondo, 56
Villa Sparina, 15066
Gavi (AT)
(39) 0143 685132
www.la-gallina.it

Osteria Lamilonga
Via Cristoforo Colombo, 10
Agliano Terme (AT)
(39) 0141 954089
www.osterialamilonga.it

Ristorante Moro
Via Mameli, 11
Asti (AT)
(39) 0141 592513
www.ristorantemoro.com

Pizzeria Ristorante Francese
Via dei Cappellai, 1
Asti (AT)
(39) 0141 592321

Ristorante Violetta
Frazione Valle San Giovanni, 1
Calamandrana (AT)
(39) 0141 769011
www.ristorantevioletta.it

Ristorante San Marco
Via Alba, 136
Canelli (AT)
(39) 0141 823544
www.sanmarcoristorante.net

Ristorante Crivello d'Oro
Via al Castello, 42
Castagnole Monferrato (AT)
(39) 0141 292237
www.ilcrivellodoro.com

Madonna della Neve
Regione Madonna delle Neve, 2
Cessole (AT)
(39) 0144 850402
www.ristorantedellaneve.it

Albergo Ristorante Garibaldi
Via Italia, 1
Cisterna d'Asti (AT)
(39) 0141 979118
www.albergoristoran
tegaribaldi.it

Le Due Lanterne
Piazza Giuseppe Garibaldi, 52
Nizza Monferrato (AT)
(39) 0141 702480

Ristorante del Belbo da Bardon
Valle Asinari, 25
San Marzano Oliveto (AT)
(39) 0141 823114

PROVINCE OF BIELLA

Al 20
Via Vignetto, 20
Biella (BI)
(039) 015 20079
www.alventi.it

Ristorante Liberty—Hotel Bugella
Via Cottolengo, 65
Biella (BI)
(039) 015 406607
www.hotelbugella.it

La Mia Crota
Via Torino, 36/C
Biella (BI)
(39) 015 30588
www.lamiacrota.it

Ristorante Baracca
Via Sant'Eusebio, 12
Biella (BI)
(39) 015 21941
www.baccaristorante.it

Osteria dell'Oca Bianca
Via Umberto I
Cavaglià (BI)
(39) 0161 185 9233
www.osteriadellocabianca.it

Il Faggio
Via Oremo, 54
Pollone (BI)
(39) 015 256 3763
www.ristoranteilfaggio.it

Ristorante Il Patio
Via Oremo, 14
Pollone (BI)
(39) 015 61568
www.ristoranteilpatio.it

PROVINCE OF CUNEO

Hotel I Castelli Ristorante
Corso Torino, 14
Alba (CN)
(39) 0173 361978
www.hotel-icastelli.com

Enoclub Ristorante
Piazza Savona, 4
Alba (CN)
(39) 0173 33994
www.caffeumberto.it

LALIBERA
Via Elvio Pertinace, 24
Alba (CN)
(39) 0173 293155
www.lalibera.com

Osteria dell'Arco
Piazza Savona, 5
Alba (CN)
(39) 0173 363974
www.osteriadellarco.it

Piazza Duomo
4, Piazza Risorgimento
12051 Alba (CN)
(39) 0173 366 167
www.piazzaduomoalba.it

Ristorante 21.9
Loc. Carretta, 4
12040 Piobesi d'Alba (CN)
(39) 0173 619261
www.ristorante21punto9.it

Antica Torre
Via Torino, 64
Barbaresco (CN)
(39) 0173 635170
www.anticatorrebarbaresco.com

Antinè Ristorante
Via Torino, 16
Barbaresco (CN)
(39) 0173 635294
www.antine.it

Ristorante Brezza
Via Lomondo, 2
Barolo (CN)
(39) 0173 560026
www.hotelbarolo.it

Buon Padre
Via delle Viole, 30
Frazione Vergne
Barolo (CN)
(39) 0173 56192
www.buon-padre.com

La Cantinetta
Via Roma, 33
Barolo (CN)
(39) 0173 56198

Osteria del Bocconvino
Via Mendicità, 14
Bra (CN)
(39) 0172 425674
www.boccondivinoslow.it

Osteria La Pimpinella
Via San Rocco, 70
Bra (CN)
(39) 333 5259801

Osteria Murivecchi
Via G. Pumiati, 19
Bra (CN)
(39) 0172 431008
www.murivecchi.it

All'Enoteca/ Osteria all'Enoteca
Via Roma, 57
Canale (CN)
(39) 0173 95857
www.davidepalluda.it

Ristorante Le Torri
Piazza Vittoria Veneto, 10
Castiglione Falletto (CN)
(39) 0173 62937
www.ristoranteletorri.it

Osteria La Torre
Via Ospedale
12062 Cherasco (CN)
(39) 0172 488458

Trattoria nelle Vigne
Via Moglia Gerlotto, 7A
12055 Diano d'Alba (CN)
(39) 0173 468503
www.trattorianellevigne.it

Osteria Battaglino
Piazza Martiri della Liberta, 12
12063 Dogliani (CN)
(39) 0173 742089
www.osteriabattaglino.it

Io e Luna
Frazione Montebello, 1
Guarene (CN)
(39) 1073 611724
www.ioeluna.com

Ristorante Bovio
Via Alba, 17
12064 La Morra (CN)
(39) 0173 590303
www.ristorantebovio.it

Massimo Camia
Strada Provinciale,
3 Alba-Barolo
La Morra (CN)
(39) 0173 56355
www.locandanelborgo.it

Fontanazza
Strada Fontanazza, 4
La Morra (CN)
(39) 0173 50718
locandafontanazza.it

Mangè
Via Roma, 3
La Morra (CN)
(39) 0173 62849
www.mange.it

Osteria Veglio
Frazione Annunziata, 9
La Morra (CN)
(39) 1073 509341
www.osteriaveglio.it

L'Osteria del Vignaiolo
Frazione Santa Maria, 12
La Morra (CN)
(39) 0173 50335
www.osteriavignaiolo.it

Da Felicin
Via Vallada, 18
Monforte d'Alba (CN)
(39)0173 78225
www.felicin.it

Trattoria della Posta
Loc. S. Anna, 87
Monforte d'Alba (CN)
(39) 0173 78120
www.trattoriadellaposta.it

Cantina dei Cacciatori
Località Villa Superiore, 59
Monteu Roero (CN)
(39) 0173 90815
www.cantinadeicacciatori.it

Cantina del Rondó
Via Fausoni
Neive (CN)
(39) 0173 679808
cantinadelrondo.it

La Contea
Piazza Contea, 8
Neive (CN)
(39) 0173 67126
www.la-contea.it

La Luna nel Pozzo
Piazza Italia, 23
Neive (CN)
(39) 0173 67098
www.lalunanelpozzo-neive.it

L'Angolo di Rosina
Piazza Caduti, 5
Novello (CN)
(39) 0173 744016
www.mangiareinlanga.it

Ristorante Il Centro
Via Umberto I, 5
Priocca d'Alba (CN)
(39) 0173 616112
www.ilcentroristorante.it

Ristorante La Crota
Via Fontana, 7
Roddi d'Alba (CN)
(39) 0173 6187

Il Vigneto
Località Ravinali, 19/20
Roddi d'Alba (CN)
(39) 0173 615630
www.ilvignetodiroddi.com

Ristorante Valentine
Via Tetti, 15
12080 San Giacomo
di Roburent (CN)
(39)0174 227013
www.valentineristorante.it

Vinoteca Centro Storico
Via Roma, 6
Serralunga d'Alba (CN)
(39) 0173 613203

Guido Ristorante
Villa Reale Fontanafredda
Via Alba, 15
12050 Serralunga d'Alba (CN)
(39) 0173 626162
www.guidoristorante.it

La Rosa dei Vini
Località Parafada, 4
Serralunga d'Alba (CN)
(39) 0173 613219
www.larosadeivini.com

Antico Podere Tota Virginia
Località Baudana, 69
Serralunga d'Alba (CN)
(39) 0173 613026
www.totavirginia.com

La Ciau del Tornavento
Piazza Baracco, 7
12050 Treiso (CN)
(39) 0173 638 333
www.laciaudeltornavento.it

Profumodivino
Viale Remembranza, 1
Treiso (CN)
(39) 0173 638017

Il Falstaff
Via Commendator Schiavino, 1
Verduno (CN)
(39) 0172 470244
www.ilfalstaff.com

Osteria San Giulio
Badia di Dulzago
Bellinzago (NO)
(39) 0321 98101
www.osteriasangiulio.it

Ristorante Arianna
Via Umberto I, 4
Cavaglietto (NO)
(39) 032 280 6134
www.ristorantearianna.it

Ristorante Convivium
Baluardo Lamarmora, 6
Novara (NO)
(39) 0321 442317
www.conviviumnovara.it

Osteria del Borgo
Via Pietro Custodi, 5
Galliate (NO)
(39) 0321 866312
http://www.osteriadelborgo.eu

**Villa Crespi—Ristorante
di Antonino Cannavacciuolo**
Via G. Fava, 18
Orta San Giulio (NO)
(39) 0322 911902
www.villacrespi.it

Ristorante Alla Torre
Via I Maggio, 75
Romagnano Sesia (NO)
(39) 0163 826411

Centro Storico, Serralunga d'Alba

Impero
Via Roma, 13
Sizzano (NO)
(39) 0321 820576
www.ristoranteimpero.eu

Al Sorriso
Via Roma, 18
Soriso (NO)
(39) 0322 983228
www.alsoriso.com

PROVINCE OF TORINO

Osteria del Paluch
Via Superga, 44
Baldissero Torinese (TO)
(39) 011 940 8750
www.ristorantepaluch.it

Ristorante La Torinese
Via Torino, 42
Baldissero Torinese (TO)
(39) 0100 946 0025
www.ristorantetorinese.it

Darmagi
Via Rivera, 7
Mercenasco (TO)
(39) 0125 710094
www.ristorantedarmagi.it

Ca' Mia
Strada Revigliasco, 138
Moncalieri (TO)
(39) 011 647 2808
www.camia.it

Frà Fiusch
Via Maurizio Beria
Revigliasco Torinese
Moncalieri Torino (TO)
(39) 011 8608224
www.frafiusch.it

Ristorante La Credenza
Via Cavour, 22
San Maurizio Canavese (TO)
(39) 011 927 8014
www.ristorantelacredenza.it

L'Acino
Via San Domenico 2/a
Torino (TO)
(39) 0111 521 7077

Osteria Antiche Sere
Via Cenischia, 9
Torino (TO)
(39) 011 385 4347

Osteria 'n Cicinin
Via Madama Cristina, 100
Torino (TO)
(39) 011 1945 4951
www.osteria-ncicinin.it

La Osteria di Pierantonio
Via Bizzozzero, 15
Torino (TO)
(39) 011 674528
www.osteriadipierantonio.it

Ristorante Consorzio
Via Monte de Pietà, 23
Torino (TO)
(39) 011 276 7661
www.ristoranteconsorzio.it

The Wines and Foods of Piemonte

Tartufi bianchi

Ristorante Al Gatto Nero
Corso Filippo Turati, 14
Torino (TO)
(39) 011 590 414
www.gattonero.it

Trattoria al Dente
Via delle Orfane, 19G
Torino (TO)
(39) 011 436 8105
www.aldentequadrilatero.com

Tre Galline
Via G. Bellezia, 37
10122 Torino (TO)
(39) 011 436 6553
www.3galline.it

Ristorante Vintage 1997
Piazza Solferino, 16H
Torino (TO)
(39) 011 535948
www.vintage1997.com

PROVINCE OF VERBANO-CUSIO-OSSOLA

Ristorante Eurossola
Piazza Matteotti 36
Domodossola (VB)
(39) 0324 481326
www.eurossola.com

Ristorante La Meridiana
Via Rosmini, 11
Domodossola (VB)
(39) 0324 240858
www.ristorantelameridiana.it

Ristorante La Stella
Brogata Baceno, 1
Domodossola (VB)
(39) 0324 248470
www.ristorantelastella.com

Antica Trattoria Pattarone
Via Gentinetta, 14
Domodossola (VB)
(39) 0324 248449
www.pattarone.com

Bottega Osteria Pulverin
Via Mizzoccola, 14
Domodossola (VB)
(39) 0324 24637
www.osteriapulverun.com

Ristorante Le Volte
Via San Vittore, 149
Intra (VB)
(39) 0323 404051

Province of Vercelli

Balin
Frazione Castell'Apertole
Castell'Apertole (VC)
(39)0161 47121
www.balinrist.it

Ristorante Franz
Via Roma, 35
Formigliana (VC)
(39) 0161 877005
www.ristorantefranz.it

Ristorante Carpe Diem
Corso Garibaldi, 244
Gattinara (VC)
(39) 0163 823778
www.ristorantecarpediem.it

Il Vigneto
Piazza Teodorico Paolotti
Gattinara (VC)
(39) 0163 834803
www.ristoranteilvigneto.it

Osteria Cascina dei Fiori
Regione Fiori
Borgo Vercelli (VC)
(39) 0161 32827

Cinzia da Christian e Manuel
Corso Magenta, 71
Vercelli (VC)
(39) 0161 253585
www.hotel-cinzia.com

Osteria Gaia
Via Thaon de Revel, 77
Vercelli, (VC)
(39) 0161 214515
www.osteriagaia.com

Giardinetto
Via Sereno, 3
Vercelli (VC)
(39) 0161 257 320
www.ilgiardinettovercelli.it

APPENDIX C

Glossary of Wine Terms

Barrique: Small oak barrel, usually about 225 liters

Botti (grandi botti): Large oak casks of various sizes, ranging from 20 to 50 HL (2000 to 5000 liters) and sometimes even larger. These have been used in Piemonte for more than a century; traditionally these were Slavonian oak, which is still used today. However there are now producers that use botti made from Austrian or French oak.

Bricco: literally "hill", often referring to the top of a hill, where vines are planted.

Cru: A single vineyard. In some zones, as in Barolo, the crus have been officially recognized. In others, the name of a cru is derived from a historical or geographical description.

doc, docg, dop: These are regulations regarding Italian wine that designate several factors, including what grape varieties can be used in which wines, minmium amount of aging, maxumum yield in the vineyards, when the wine can be released, and several other factors. I have opted not to dwell too long on these terms in this book, as the original significance of DOCG (*Denominazione di Origine Controllata e Garantita*), representing the finest Italian wines—such as Barolo and Barbaresco in Piemonte—has been dumbed down to the point of too many wines being awarded DOCG status (Asti Spumante is a prime example; the best are very nice wines, but hardly among the finest in Italy). DOP refers to *Denominazione di Origine Protetta*, a catch all category that includes DOC and DOCG.

Passito: A sweet wine in which the grapes have been naturally dried after harvest, often in a temperature-controlled room.

Sorì: Top of a hill, south facing, so that it receives ample sunshine. This term is used for several wines, including the finest Dolcetto from Diano d'Alba.

Sottozona: subzone

Vigna Vecchia: Old Vine (plural, *vigne vecchie*)

Vendemmia: harvest

APPENDIX D

Foods of Piemonte

A Few Classic Examples

Agnolotti del Plin (dal Plin, al Plin): Classic Piemontese handmade
pasta. Small, square ravioli; *plin* means "to pinch," named as the
shape and size makes it easy to pinch with two fingers.

Bagna Cauda: A sauce or dip with garlic, anchovies and oil.

Bollito Misto: Boiled meats

Bunet (Bonet): A pudding-like dessert comprised of several ingredients, often including rum, sugar, eggs, chocolate and hazelnuts.

Cardo Gobbo: A member of the artichoke family, this white vegetable
is often used as an ingredient in *bagna cauda*; it is extremely
high in nutritional value.

Carne cruda: Raw beef served with lemon juice and olive oil; a classic antipasto in Piemonte.

Coniglio brasato: Braised rabbit

Crostata: Tart; often filled with fruit.

Finanziera: A dish that defines the Italian manner of using every
part of an animal, this is comprised of such ingredients as
sweetbreads, cock's combs and veal brains, along with mushrooms, garlic and clove.

Faraona: Guinea hen

Fassone: Piemontese beef; often used for *carne cruda*

Guancia di vitello brasata: Braised veal cheeks

Nocciole: Hazelnuts

Riso Venere: One of the most distinctive types of rice grown in the
provinces of Novara and Vercelli, Riso Venere is a black rice that
is a cross between a black rice from China and a local Piemontese strain.

Robiola di Roccaverano: Named for the town of Roccaverano in the
province of Asti, this is a soft-ripened cheese made exclusively
from goat's milk or a mixture of goat and sheep milk.

Salsiccia di Bra: Pork and beef sausage (sometimes veal) from the town of Bra and nearby communes—very traditional; often served as an antipasto.

Tajarin (Tagliolini): Very, thin, long handmade pasta that is renowned in the region. The classic version today is made from 40 egg yolks. *Tajarin* is often served with a meat sauce or a butter sauce.

Tartufi Bianchi: The famed white truffles of Alba, arguably the most famous and expensive truffles in the world. These are harvested in October and November; the Alba Truffle festival takes place from mid-October to mid-November.

Toma: Cow's milk cheese, creamy and mild, this is one of the region's most famous cheeses.

Vitello Tonnato: Thinly sliced raw veal served cold with a thick tuna sauce similar in consistency to mayonnaise.

ACKNOWLEDGEMENTS

Writing this book would not have been possible without the graciousness of dozens of individuals in Piemonte; first and foremost, the producers. Every vintner I met was of great help, taking the time to answer my seemingly endless questions about their wines and land; among the most generous included Anna Maria Abbona; Giuseppino Anfossi; Raffaella Bologna; Nicoletta Bocca; Alessandro Ceretto; Luca Currado; Danilo Drocco; Claudio Fenocchio; Valter Fissore; Sergio Germano; Christoph Kunzli; Alessandro Locatelli; Paolo and Luisella Manzone; Franco Massolino; Mariacristina Oddero; Massimo Pastura; Pietro Ratti; Paola Rinaldi; Giovanna Rizzolio; Aldo Vacca; Gianni Voerzio, and Roberto Voerzio.

Thank you to a few Italian wine journalists who helped me learn so much in Piemonte; including Roberto Giuliani and Carlo Macchi.

I also want to thank the public relations people in Piemonte (and elsewhere) who greatly aided me in my travels around the region; Annalisa Chiavazza and Marta Sobrino were most helpful.

Thanks also to the chefs and restaurateurs for not only inspiring me with their imaginative cuisine, but also for taking the time to answer to my inquiries; a special thank you to Flavia Boffa of LALIBERA in Alba and Alessio Cighetti of Centro Storico in Serralunga d'Alba.

Thank you to Jerry Alt and Annette Kerstin Pasko for their assistance with photography as well as the wonderful portrait on the back cover, and thanks to Mick Rock for his technical support on my photos. Mick, I appreciate the encouragement!

Thank you to Diana Zahuranec for her advice on several wines and producers that I was not familiar with before I started this project; thanks also to her for promoting my work.

Finally, a heartfelt thank you to Alessandro Masnaghetti, not only for his beautiful maps that are part of this book, but also for his friendship, as he aided me in numerous ways and made me feel most welcome in Piemonte.

BIBLIOGRAPHY

Note that this list is brief, as 99.9% of this book is based on personal visits and interviews with producers, chefs and other individuals in Piemonte.

If you are looking to learn more about the wines, grapes and vineyards of Piemonte, these are noteworthy books.

Bastianich, Joseph and Lynch, David. *Vino Italiano: The Regional Wines of Italy.* New York: Clarkson Potter, 2002

D'Agata, Ian. *Native Wine Grapes of Italy.* Berkeley and Los Angeles, CA: University of California Press, 2014

Masnaghetti, Alessandro. *Barolo mga: Menzioni Geografiche Aggiuntive.* Enogea, 2015

O'Keefe, Kerin. *Barolo and Barbaresco: The King and Queen of Italian Wine.* Berkeley and Los Angeles, CA, 2014

INDEX

The Wines and Foods of Piemonte

Made in the USA
Monee, IL
11 November 2020